# A Victorian Housebuilder's Guide

## "WOODWARD'S NATIONAL ARCHITECT"
## OF 1869

*George E. Woodward and*
*Edward G. Thompson*

DOVER PUBLICATIONS, INC., *New York*

Published in Canada by General Publishing Company, Ltd., 30 Lesmill Road, Don Mills, Toronto, Ontario.

Published in the United Kingdom by Constable and Company, Ltd., 10 Orange Street, London WC2H 7EG.

This Dover edition, first published in 1988, is an unabridged republication of the work originally published by Geo. E. Woodward, New York, in 1869 under the title *Woodward's National Architect*. The advertisements that appeared at the end of the original volume have been omitted in the present edition.

Manufactured in the United States of America
Dover Publications, Inc., 31 East 2nd Street, Mineola, N.Y. 11501

**Library of Congress Cataloging-in-Publication Data**

Woodward, George E. (George Evertson), 1829–1905.
  A Victorian housebuilder's guide.

  Reprint. Originally published: Woodward's national architect. New York : G. E. Woodward, 1869.
  1. Architecture, Domestic—United States—Designs and plans. I. Thompson, Edward G.   II. Title.
[NA7205.W66   1988]   728.3′7′0222        88-3989
ISBN 0-486-25704-5

# Woodward's
# National Architect

## BY

## GEO. E. WOODWARD, ARCHITECT,

## &

## Edward G. Thompson, Architect.

1000
Designs, Plans & Details
Engraved & printed by KORFF BROS. New York.

*[Original decorative title page]*

# WOODWARD'S
# NATIONAL ARCHITECT;

CONTAINING

## 1000 ORIGINAL DESIGNS, PLANS AND DETAILS,

## 𝔗o 𝔚orking 𝔖cale,

FOR THE

## PRACTICAL CONSTRUCTION OF DWELLING HOUSES

FOR THE

## COUNTRY, SUBURB AND VILLAGE.

WITH

## FULL AND COMPLETE SETS OF SPECIFICATIONS AND AN ESTIMATE OF THE COST OF EACH DESIGN.

BY

## GEO. E. WOODWARD, ARCHITECT,

Author of "Woodward's Country Homes," "Woodward's Cottages and Farm-Houses," Woodward's Suburban and Country Houses," Etc.,

AND

## EDWARD G. THOMPSON, ARCHITECT.

## NEW YORK:
### GEO. E. WOODWARD, 191 BROADWAY.

*[Original full title page and imprint]*

# INTRODUCTION.

In presenting to the public a new work on Architecture, we have endeavored to occupy a field not hitherto covered in a similar manner, and also to fulfill a demand that has been made on us for some years past for practical working plans adapted to the wants of the great mass of the inhabitants of our country—plans, elevations, working details, estimates, and specifications so clearly made out and so thoroughly and practically prepared, that they may at once be placed in the hands of a builder for execution.

The plan of this work embraces designs for houses of moderate valuations, estimated at New York prices as a basis, with such detail prices as will enable one to ascertain the cost in his own locality by comparison with the different rates of prices that always exist in different sections of the country.

The forms of specifications given are such, that they may be adapted to any of the designs, so that full and final estimates can be obtained from local builders. They will also serve as hints for the preparation of specifications for any class of dwelling houses.

Front and side elevations, plans and detail drawings to working scale are given for each design, and in many cases perspective views are shown. In addition, we have added a large number of miscellaneous details which will enable any one to select such styles of finish as he may prefer.

The drawings are so carefully made and figured as to explain thoroughly their meaning without further description than that found necessary in the specifications, and we have, therefore, carefully avoided all theories, essays, or speculations on the subject, believing we can convey more practical and valuable information by carefully-executed drawings than by whole volumes of descriptive matter. From a long experience as Architect, author and publisher, we believe this work will fully meet the popular demand, and be found alike indispensable to those who propose the erection of buildings, as well as to all classes of mechanics engaged in their construction.

We are indebted to Mr. SAMUEL F. EVELETH, Architect, N. Y., for designs on Plates Nos. 70 and 71, and Miscellaneous Details on Plates numbered 82 to 88, and 90 to 96.

# WOODWARD'S NATIONAL ARCHITECT.

## DESCRIPTION OF PLATES.

### ALL DRAWN TO WORKING SCALE.

Estimates made in accordance with New York price list given on another page, which must be altered to suit local prices wherever used.

DESIGN No. 1. *Plate* No. 1. Perspective view of Dwelling House. To cost $7,000.
" " 2. Front and side elevation. $\frac{1}{16}$-inch scale.
" " 3. First and second floor plans, " "
" " 4. Section of house and details, to $\frac{1}{2}$-inch scale.
Carpenters' Specification in full.
Masons' " "
Plumbers' " "

DESIGN No. 2. *Plate* No. 5. Perspective view, French-roof Cottage. To cost $5,000.
" " 6. Front elevation. $\frac{1}{8}$-inch scale.
Right side elevation. $\frac{1}{16}$-inch scale.
" " 7. Left side elevation. $\frac{1}{16}$-inch scale.
First and second floor plans. $\frac{1}{16}$-inch scale.
" " 8. Section of house. $\frac{1}{8}$-inch scale.
Details. $\frac{1}{2}$-inch scale.
" " 9. Details of front bay window, dormer, etc.

DESIGN No. 3. *Plate* No. 10. Perspective view of Small Cottage. To cost $2,000.
" " 11. Front and side elevations. $\frac{1}{8}$-inch scale.

DESCRIPTION OF PLATES.

DESIGN No. 12.   *Plate* No. 54.   First and second floor plans
             "    "  55.   Details in full to scale.

DESIGN No. 13.   *Plate* No. 56.   Front and side elevations of Cottage ½-inch scale. To cost $4,700.
             "    "  57.   First and second floor plans.
             "    "  58.   Details in full to scale.

DESIGN No. 14.   *Plate* No. 59.   Front and side elevations of Stable.   To cost $2,500.
             "    "  60.   Floor plan and details to scale.

DESIGN No. 15.   *Plate* No. 61.   Front elevation of Cottage.   To cost $6,000.
             "    "  62.   Side elevation to scale.
             "    "  63.   First floor plan.
             "    "  64.   Second floor plan.
             "    "  65.   Details to working scale.
             "    "  66.   Details to working scale.

DESIGN No. 16.   *Plate* No. 67.   Suburban City House for lot 50 feet front. To cost $6,000.
             "    "  68.   First and second floor plans.
             "    "  69.   Details to scale.

DESIGN No. 17.   *Plate* No. 70.   Front and side elevations for City House for lot 50 feet front. French roof and three floor plans.   To cost $5,000.
Masons' specification in full.
Carpenters' specification in full.

DESIGN No. 18.   Plate No. 71.   Suburban City House, French roof, front and side elevations, and three floor plans.   To cost $5,000.

DESIGN No. 19.   *Plate* No. 72.   Front elevation of Ornamental Brick Villa, with French roof and tower.   To cost $30,000. Designed for erection at Rutherfurd Heights on the Passaic River, N. J.

# PRICES OF BUILDING MATERIALS AND LABOR,

## AT NEW YORK, JANUARY, 1869.

Estimates in this work are based on the prices here given, and cost of erection in other localities will be fixed by the local prices of materials.

MASON WORK AND MATERIALS.

Stone wall, including all materials, laid dry, per foot 23 cents.
do    do laid with mortar,    -    -    do  23  do.
Excavation, per cubic yard,    -    -    -    40  do.
Brick, per thousand, laid.  Pale, $19 50 to $23 50.  Hard burned, $21 to $25.
Cement, per barrel, $2 50 to $3.
Lime,    do    $1 75.
Hair, per bushel,    70 cents.
Lath and plastering, including all materials, 1 coat, per square yard, 40 cents.
    do    do    do    2 coats,    do    60  do.
    do    do    do    3 coats,    do    70  do.
Laths, per thousand, $3 50 to $4 50.

Prices for all the timber, covering, flooring and finishing lumber, per thousand feet, board measure.

FRAMING TIMBER.

Pine, $45.  Sawed to order.  Spruce, $25.  Sawed to order.
Hemlock, $22 to $25.
Firring, 2 inches wide, 6 cents each.
Studding, 13 feet by 2 × 4 inches, 21 cents each.  3 × 4, 24 cents each.
Shingles, $8 to $10.

ROOFING.

Hemlock, 1 inch thick, $24 per thousand.
Pine, 1¼ inches thick, matched, $45 per thousand.
Spruce,    do    do    $35    do
Slating, per square of 100 feet, metal extra.  1st quality of slates, $15.  2d quality, $14.
Tinning, per square of 100 feet, $11 to $13.
Leaders, 4 inches calibre, per lineal foot, 30 cents.

FLOORING.

Spruce, 5 inches wide, 1¼-inch thick, $35 per thousand, planed and matched.
Spruce, 10 inches wide, 1¼-inch thick, planed and matched, $35 per thousand,
White pine, 5 inches wide, as above, $45.
White pine, 10 inches wide, as above, $45.
Georgia pine, 3 to 5 inches wide, $60 to $80, 1¼-inch thick, planed and matched.
Hemlock, 1-inch thick, matched, $24.

FINISHING STOCK, SEASONED.

Clear white pine, $65 per thousand.
Second quality of clear pine, $40 to $50.

HARDWARE.

Nails, per cwt., $5 75.

LABOR PER DAY.

| | | | |
|---|---|---|---|
| Stone Mason, $4 00. | Mason's Tender, $3 00. | |
| Bricklayer, 5 00. | Carpenter, 3 75. | |
| Plasterer, 5 50. | Painter, 3 50. | Laborer, $2 00. |

Engr & print by KORFF BROTHERS 54 William St N Y

Design No. I.

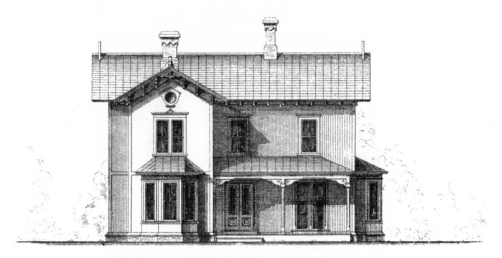

— Front Elevation. —

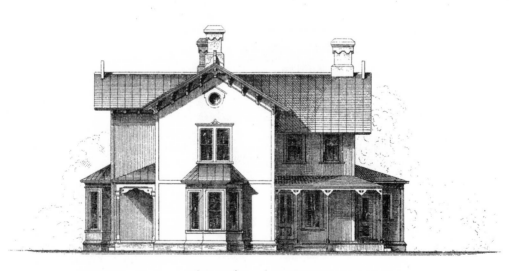

— Side Elevation. —

Scale. 1/16 Inch to One Foot.

Design No. 1.                                    Plate No. 3.

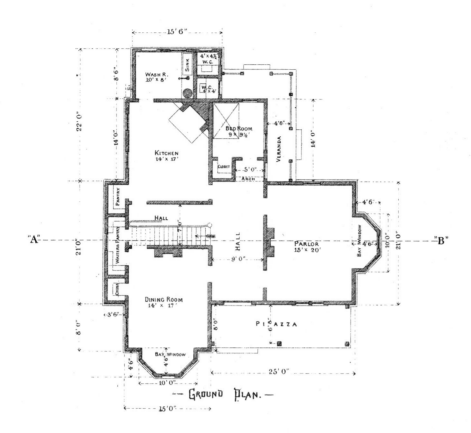

— Ground Plan. —

— Chamber Plan. —

Scale. 1/16 Inch to One Foot.

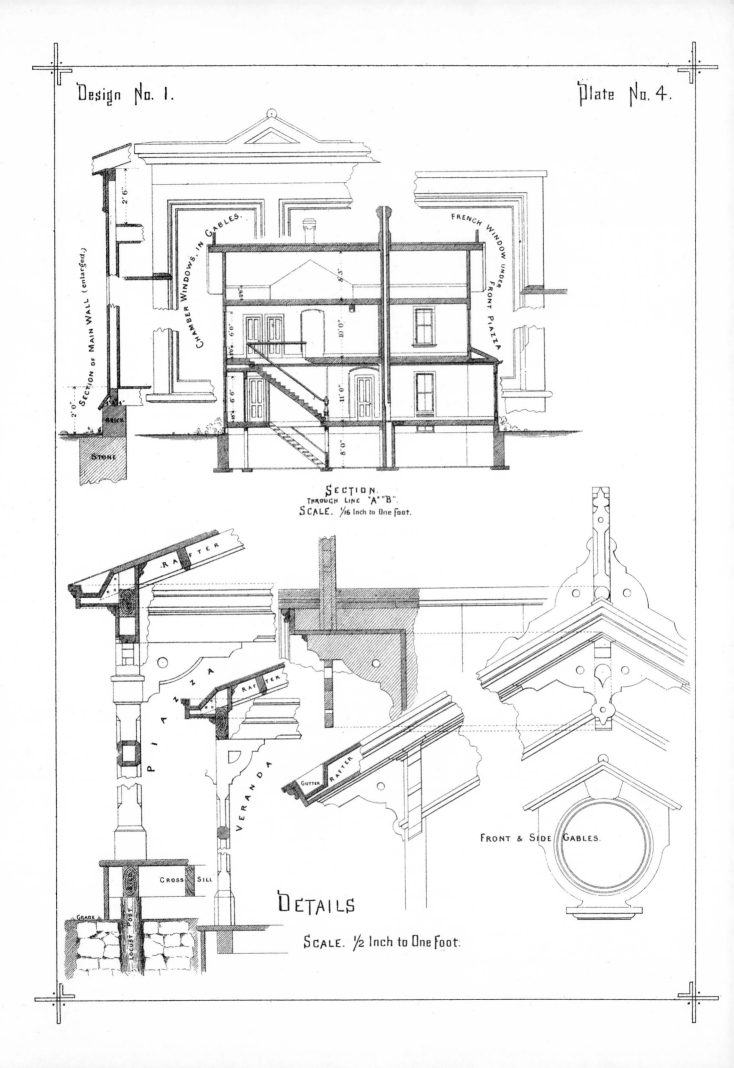

Design No. 1.

Plate No. 4.

2'6"

SECTION OF MAIN WALL (enlarged.)

CHAMBER WINDOWS. IN GABLES.

FRENCH WINDOW UNDER FRONT PIAZZA

8'3"

2'6"

6'0"

10'0"

11'0"

6'6"

2'0"

3'4"

BRICK

STONE

8'0"

SECTION.
THROUGH LINE "A"."B".
SCALE. 1/16 Inch to One Foot.

RAFTER

PIAZZA

RAFTER

VERANDA

GUTTER RAFTER

FRONT & SIDE GABLES.

GRADE

LOCUST POST.

CROSS SILL

DETAILS

SCALE. 1/2 Inch to One Foot.

# DESIGN No. 1.

# CARPENTERS' SPECIFICATION.

———◆■◆———

DIMENSIONS, ETC.  For Dimensions, heights of stories and internal arrangement of the building, see drawings.

The figures on the drawings to be followed in the construction in all cases in preference to measurement by the scale.

## TIMBERING.

QUALITY OF TIM-  Furnish all the Timber used in the construction, of good sound square-
BER.  edged quality, free from any and every imperfection tending to impair its durability or strength, and as well seasoned as any convenient market will afford.  The Sills, Posts, Floor Joist and Rafters, to be of Chesnut, Pine or Spruce, and the remaining framing timber of Hemlock, Pine or Spruce, at the option of the Contractor.

DIMENSIONS  of the Timber, as follows:

Sills,              9 × 4 inches.
Angle Posts,        8 × 4  do
Intermediate  do  6 × 4  do
Girts,              6 × 4  do
Plates, (main building,)     6 × 4 inches.
   do    (Wash Room Extension,)    4 × 4 inches.
Valley Rafters,          7 × 4  do
Common   do              6 × 3  do (20 inches from centres.)
Carriage Beams and Headers, 4 inches thick.

| | | |
|---|---|---|
| Braces (long,) | | 4 × 4 inches. |
| do (short,) | | 4 × 3 do |
| Nailing Joist, (16 inches from centres.) | 4 × 2 do | |
| Floor Joist. 1st, tier, ⎫ | | 9 × 2 do |
| do 2d, do ⎬ 16 inches from centres, | 10 × 2 do | |
| do 3d, do ⎭ | | 8 × 2 do |
| Girder in Cellar, | 5 × 5 do | |

BRIDGING.     Cut in one row of cross bridging in each tier of Beams.

FRAMING.     Execute all the framing in a workmanlike and thoroughly substantial manner, and in strict accordance with the requirements of the design.

Double the Beams where the partitions bear on them.

Cut the lower end of the Rafters where projecting beyond the Plate, as required by the detail drawings.

Nail the Braces in bare-foot.

Support the Rafters, centrally, as hereinafter described under the head of "PARTITIONS AND FIRRING."

Support the Cellar Girders (under the floor-bearing partitions) on Locust posts, to average about 4 feet apart.

| | |
|---|---|
| PIAZZA AND VER-   Outside Sills and Cross Sills (at each post), | 6 × 4 inches. |
| ANDA FRAMING.   Floor Joist (2 feet from centres), | 6 × 2 do |
| Plates (Piazza), cased all around, | 7 × 4 do |
| do (Veranda), | S × 3 do |
| Rafters, | 4 × 2 do |

The Rafters planed three sides with 1¼-inch half round, nailed to bottom edge, as per details.

Support the floor upon locust posts set 3 feet in the ground.

## EXTERIOR WORK.

ROOF PLANKING,     Cover the Piazza and Veranda roofs, with 1¼-inch perfectly sound, narrow plank, planed side down (planed smooth)—*no beads.*

ETC.     Cover all other roofs, with 1-inch tongued lumber, free from rot and holes.

Case up for and finish a 2 × 3-feet scuttle in the roof, and provide with

2

tongued plank cover, hinged with strong butts, and fastened with hook and staple.

Case up the ends of the rafters, and form the gutters as shcwn by the drawings. The Cornice soffit to be sheathed with narrow ⅞-inch beaded sheathing.

TINNING.     Cover all the roofs and line the gutters with charcoal roof tin I. C. brand, the sheets nailed, clenched and white leaded in the best manner and laid with the standing lock joint.

Extend the tin well into the joints of the brick chimneys, and where the Piazza and other roofs abut against the siding, at least 6 inches up behind the boards. Nail strips of tin on top of window casings—watertight.

Furnish all the required leaders of sufficient size to convey the water from the gutters to the cistern and the tank in attic. Put up said leaders, with neat, ornamental, galvanized iron holdfasts.

FINIALS, ETC.     Provide the ridges with 3-inch roll moulding, covering the same with Zinc, and finish with scroll-sawed finials at the gable terminations.

WEATHER BOARDING.     Cover the exterior of the frame with first class clear clapboards, showing a uniform weathering and rebated in no case less than ¾ inch.

CORNER BOARDS.     Furnish the angles with 5 × 5 × 1¼-inch returned corner boards.

WATER TABLE.     Put on 1½-inch canted water-table, rebating over the underpinning and tonguing under the siding, as per drawings.

CORNICES, ETC.     Provide the eave and gable cornices with sawed brackets (4 inches thick), architrave and bed moulds, and scroll-sawed gable pendents, 2 inches thick.

DOOR AND WINDOW CASINGS.     Case all the doors and windows on the outside with 1¼-inch casings, corniced as shown by the drawings, and provide the windows with 2-inch sills.

PIAZZA FINISH.     Case up the piazza columns and furnish with caps and bases as shown. Cut in 2¾-inch brackets, form cornice, and mould all as per drawings.

Plane up and chamfer the small columns of veranda and provide with brackets, etc., as per details.

Lay the piazza and veranda floors with narrow, clear 1¼-inch tongued flooring, blind nailed, joints laid in white lead.

Firr out from the sills, and case underneath the floors down to the grade level as shown.

OUTSIDE STEPS.    Build the outside steps and platforms as drawn, with 1¼-inch nosed treads, and 1-inch risers and facias.  Provide with cove moulding underneath the nosings of front steps.

## FLOORING.

Lay the attic floor with wide, perfectly sound 1-inch tongued lumber nailed twice to each bearing.

Lay all the remaining floors throughout, with narrow 1¼-inch tongued flooring, free from defects and blind nailed.

Flush off all the joints of the floors with the plane.

Cut in 2 × ½-inch borders around all the hearths.

Furnish all the doors with hard wood saddles.

## PARTITIONS AND FIRRING.

Set all the partitions that support beams, with 3 × 4-inch hemlock, 12 inches from centers, with 3 × 4-inch plates, (sound, straight and square edged,) and 3 × 4-inch sills.  Form all the angles solid, and set all door studs double.

Set studs of 3 × 4-inch hemlock, with 4 × 4-inch plate, and 3 × 4-inch sills, 4 feet apart, to support rafters in attic.

BRIDGING.    Bridge all the Partitions once in their height.

FIRRING.    Cross-firr the 1st, and 2d, story ceilings, with 1-inch strip firring, and also firr the closet and bath room ceilings (under tank) down level, 8 feet high in the clear.

Firr off for the segmental arches across halls.  Do any other firring required by the design.

Set grounds to all openings and leave them on.

## STAIRS.

TO CELLAR.    Build stairs to cellar, with 1½-inch strings, and 1¼-inch treads. (no risers) planed up and mortised together. Case up around the well-hole at the top to receive the plastering, and provide the steps with pine slat-rail.

**To Scuttle.** Build step-ladder reaching from attic floor to scuttle, with 1¼-inch lumber, neatly planed up and grooved together.

**To Attic.** Build the attic stairs, with 1¼-inch strings and treads, with enclosed soffit, and open risers. Enclose through servant's closet, from string to ceiling, with ⅞-inch vertical beaded sheathing.

**To Chambers.** **Principal flight.** Build the principal flight of stairs from main to chamber hall, with 1¼-inch strings and treads, and 1-inch risers and facias; the steps front and back tongued. Return and mould the nosings, and mould the front string in a tasteful manner. Finish the wall string in correspondence with the base in the halls, and support the whole on 6×4-inch timbers rough bracketed to each tread. Surmount with 4½×3-inch toad-back moulded rail, 1⅞-inch fancy turned ballusters of selected pattern, and provide with 8-inch octagon-turned and veneered newel, at the start. The rail, ballusters and newel to be of the best sound seasoned Black Walnut, oiled two coats, and well rubbed down at the completion.

## WINDOWS AND GLASS.

**Frames.** Make the mullion window frame in parlor front, with box-head, and all other frames throughout, (above the cellar,) the usual box frames for double hanging the sash, with 2-inch best pulleys, iron weights and hemp cord.

Make the Cellar frames with 2-inch plank rebated for the sash to be hinged and opened upwards; the sash 1½-inch thick.

**Sashes.** Make the attic frames and sash in the same manner; the sash to be hinged to open horizontally. Fasten these sash shut, with bolts, and open, with buttons.

Make the sash in wash room, and the small sashes in water closet 1½-inch thick, and all other window sash throughout, 1¾-inch thick.

**Glass.** Glaze all the windows throughout, with the first quality of French sheet glass.

Glaze the upper panels of main entrance doors with the best quality of French polished plate glass, and the same panels in the rear hall door opening on veranda, with enameled glass of selected pattern.

# DOORS.

THICKNESS.    Make the front doors 2 inches thick, as per elevation and working drawings.

The 1st story principal room doors, 1¾ inch thick, and all other doors throughout, 1½ inch thick.

PANELS.    Make all the doors four panels each, and double face with mouldings.

HEIGHT.    Make the parlor doors, 7 feet 9 inches in height, the remaining 1st story room doors, 7 feet 4 inches high, and all other doors throughout, 7 feet in height.

The width of the doors to vary as their several situations require, and as indicated on the plans.

HINGING.    Hinge all the doors on the best quality of iron butts, of the size respectively required.

BOLTS.    Put two wrought iron tail bolts, (long and short,) on the standing front, folding door, and two 8-inch malleable iron bolts on each other outside door.

LOCKS.    Put a 6½-inch mortise lock on the front door, with night latch and keys and bronzed medallion furniture.

5-inch mortise locks on the 1st and 2d stories, principal room doors, with bronzed medallion furniture in the main hall parlor and dining room, and white porcelain furniture on the remainder.

Put 5-inch rim locks on all other doors throughout with dark mineral furniture.

All the locks to be of the best and most approved manufacture.

SASH FASTEN-
INGS.    Fasten all the sash throughout when not otherwise specified with the most approved sash fastenings, corresponding in style with the lock furniture of the rooms in which they are situated.

# BELLS.

Put up with copper wire in zinc tubes in a thorough workmanlike manner, the following gong bells. The pulls respectively to correspond in style of finish with the neighboring door furniture.

One pull from front door to kitchen.

|     |     |                   |     |
| --- | --- | ----------------- | --- |
| do  | do  | dining room       | do  |
| do  | do  | library           | do  |
| do  | do  | parlor            | do  |
| do  | do  | 2d story hall     | do  |
| do  | do  | principal chamber to servants room in attic. | |

## INSIDE FINISH.

TRIMMINGS,
BASE, ETC.

Trim all the doors with 1¼-inch jambs, and all the doors and windows throughout the first and chamber stories of the main building, with neat moulded architraves, 7 inches wide below, and 5 inches above. Trim throughout the kitchen wing, and in all closets, with plain chamfered architraves 4½ inches wide.

All the windows in principal rooms, to be trimmed down to the floors with framed, moulded and paneled backs, and elsewhere throughout on nosing sills with moulded aprons.

Put down 8-inch plain moulded base in the principal rooms of 1st story, 6½-inch do. in chambers, and 6-inch plain chamfered plinth elsewhere throughout (where not wainscoted). All the base to tongue down ⅜-inch into a moulded carpet strip, rebated to receive it.

WAINSCOT.

Wainscot the walls of the kitchen and wash room, 3 feet in height above the floor, with ⅞-inch clear, tongued and beaded sheathing, 4-inch wide, and neatly cap.

BATH ROOM.

Case up the bath-tub and water-closet with Black Walnut, and tongue down a plain beveled surbase over against the wall. Hinge both flap and seat of water-closet, with brass butts. Case up the wash-basin in a similar manner, enclosed below with paneled door, hinged on brass butts and fastened with snap-lock.

Build raised platform 8 inches in height, on which to set bath tub and water-closet, as indicated on the plans.

TANK.

Construct a tank in attic, over the bath room, 6 feet 6 inches long, by 5 feet 4 inches wide, and 3 feet deep, framed in a substantial manner with

3 × 4-inch and 2 × 4-inch joist, lined with 1¼-inch tongued plank. The whole to be suspended upon 14 × 4-inch beams bearing upon main partition and in-tertie, and framed with headers of the same size over the partitions. The bottom of the tank to be firred and plastered in the bath room, finishing 7 feet 6 inches in the clear above the floor.

SHELVES, HOOKS, ETC.    Shelve the closets and pantries as indicated on the plans and otherwise required, with clear lumber planed smooth, and put up the required number of double iron clothes-hooks. Both hooks and shelves to be fastened on neatly moulded cleets mitred at the angles.

Fit up each end of the waiters' pantry, with counter shelf, and two dovetailed drawers, as indicated on the drawing. Also provide kitchen pan-try with two dovetailed drawers.

WOODEN MAN-TELS.    Put up in two of the chambers, neat wooden mantels of the design selected by the owner from the examples herein given. The lumber used to be perfectly clear.

CUTTING, ETC.    Do any necessary cutting, mending, and repairing, required by the work of gasfitters, plumbers, bell-hangers, and others.

## OUTSIDE BLINDS.

Furnish plain outside blinds for all windows (except cellar and attic); hinged on best blind hinges and fastened with approved patent fastenings

## PAINTING.

Properly stop with oil putty, all nail holes and other imperfections in the work to be painted, and size all exposed knots, etc.

Paint all the wood work of the building outside and inside, (exclusive of the inside floors, and inclusive of the piazza floors and outside steps, and the cutting in of the stairs) two good coats of the best English white lead and oil paint. Also, paint the kitchen fire-place, the chimney shafts, and the brick underpinning where exposed to view, two coats.

Thoroughly cleanse the tin roofs and gutters, and paint two coats of best metallic roof paint.

Grain the wood-work in kitchen and wash room, in imitation of light oak.

Finish all the work in color, as directed by the owner, or his appointed superintendent.

CLEANSING.     Remove all waste material and rubbish accumulated by the carpenter, at the completion, and leave the building and premises thoroughly clean; scrub the floors, and wash the windows.

## MATERIALS, ETC.

LUMBER.     Furnish all the lumber of white pine where not otherwise specified, of good sound quality, and as well seasoned as the market affords. All the sashes, panel work and interior trimmings to be of clear lumber.

The entire work to be completely finished in the best manner of the style specified.

Any work exhibited by the drawings to be executed by the contractor, though unmentioned herein.

# MASONS' SPECIFICATION.

## DESIGN No. 1.

———◆•◆•◆———

## EXCAVATING.

Do all the necessary excavating for the cellar, dwarf wall under laundry extension, cistern, cesspool and sink. Grade the excavated earth around the building as may be directed.

Lay aside the top soil and sods at the commencement, and replace over the graded surface at the completion.

## WALLING.

STONE WALLS, ETC.

Build the cellar and foundation walls of good building stone, of flat bed and firm build, laid in hydraulic ground lime, and sharp, clean sand mortar. Lay down substantial flat-stone foundations under the chimneys, and girder posts in the cellar.

Lay down a flat stone not less than 18 inches diameter under the piazza locust under-posts, bedded below the action of the frost. Fill in around the posts up to the grade level with small broken stone packed in dry.

Lay down footings under all the walls of the building, of flat stones not less than 2 feet long and 6 inches thick, bedded cross-wise of the walls on the natural undisturbed earth. Build the walls from thence up to the grade in height, by and full to a line on the inner face, and flush and point at the completion. These walls to average 20 inches in thickness—the greater breadth at the base.

PRIVY-SINK.

Stone up the privy sink, 8 feet deep, of the size shown on the plans.

and line with 4 inches brick work. Flush the inner face smoothly with hydraulic cement, and connect with cesspool through earthen drain pipe properly trapped.

CESSPOOL, ETC.    Stone up a cesspool 3 feet in diameter and 8 feet deep, covered with a 3-inch rough flag, provided with man-hole, etc., complete.

Make the necessary connections with the cistern to receive the overflow, through earthen pipe of the required size.

BRICK-WORK.    Build the wall from the top of the cellar stone walls, 16 inches in height, and 12 inches thick. These walls to be flush with the stone walls on which they bear, on the inner face, and the joints flushed full and rubbed for painting on the exterior, where exposed to view.

Build the brick walls under sills of laundry extension the same height and 8 inches thick; these walls to bear upon the centre of the dwarf-foundation walls below. Finish the exterior face as above described.

CHIMNEYS.    Build the chimneys, ash pits, etc., as per plan. Build a ventilating flue in the kitchen, and provide for registers in the kitchen and bath room. Strike the joints and smoothly parget all the flues. Top out above the roof as per drawings, with selected brick cut where required and prepared for painting. Face the throat, jambs and breast, of the kitchen fire-place, with selected brick prepared for painting.

Turn trimmer arches against all the hearths, and furnish the required rough brick, mortar and plaster for setting the mantels, hearths and range.

CISTERN.    Build a cistern where directed, 10 feet diameter and 10 feet deep, with 8-inch walls, 4-inch arch and neck, and 5-inch bottom, (two courses on the flat,) the whole laid in and smoothly coated on the inside with cement. Lay a strong rough flag over man-hole in the neck. Connect the cistern with house leaders, through 5-inch vitrified pipe laid in below the action of the frost.

All the above mentioned brick work to be built with the best quality of hard-burnt common brick, laid in strong mortar formed with the usual materials for first class work.

11

NOGGING.    Fill in the entire frame of the building below the attic floor, with pale brick, laid on edge in mortar; all joints flushed full.

## BLUE-STONE.

KITCHEN HEARTH.    Furnish a rubbed blue stone kitchen hearth, of the size shown on the plans, and not less than 4 inches thick; also, provide a lintel for the fireplace, 5 feet 6 inches long, 8 inches rise, and 4 inches bed.

WINDOW SILLS.    Provide the cellar windows, with 4-inch blue stone axed sills, of 5 inches bed and the required length.

FLAGS.    Provide smoothly dressed flags, 2 feet wide by the required length, at the foot of the outside entrance steps.

## PLASTERING.

Lath the cellar ceiling, and the walls and ceilings of the 1st and 2nd stories, with the best quality of dry seasoned lath, securely nailed to each stud, and joints broke every sixth lath.

Plaster the cellar ceiling one good coat, and the remaining walls and ceilings, where lathed, three coats—scratch, brown and hard-finish—with the very best materials in use.

CORNICES.    Run neat moulded cornices of about 5 inches rise, and 8 inches projection, in the parlor, main hall and dining room.

CENTRES.    Put up small enriched centres of such pattern as the owner may select.

ANGLE BEADS.    Plaster small return beads on all exposed plaster angles, splayed off at the top and bottom.

ARCHES.    Finish the segmental arches in the main and chamber halls, with 2-inch Boutelle moulding on the soffit angles as shown by the detail drawings.

Excepting behind the kitchen wainscot, the plastering in all cases to extend up to the grounds and down to the floors.

REMOVAL OF RUBBISH, ETC.    The entire Masons' work to be delivered up in thoroughly good order and repair at the completion, and all of the Masons' waste material and rubbish accumulated during the progress of the work, to be removed from the premises, or disposed about them, at the option of the owner.

# DESIGN No. 1.

# PLUMBERS' SPECIFICATION.

———————— ▸•◂•▸•◂ ————————

Specification of the Plumbing Work and materials required in erecting House per Design No. 1.

IRON SOIL PIPE.    Furnish and connect with privy sink a 4-inch cast-iron soil pipe, and extend the same up and behind the kitchen flue a sufficient height above the 2d story floor to receive the overflow from the tank. Connect with water-closet in bath-room through 4-inch lead soil pipe, weighing not less than 6 pounds to the foot, properly trapped. Put up the iron pipe with iron holdfasts, and caulk all the joints water-tight with lead.

SUPPLY PIPE.    Furnish a ¾-inch B lead supply pipe and connect with the attic tank, and extend it down and connect it with the boiler in kitchen.

BOILER.    Furnish and set on iron stand in wash-room where shown on the plans, a 40-gallon copper boiler, round head and riveted, well hooked, soldered, and smoothly planished. Connect the same with the brass pipes of the water-back of the range by 1-inch copper pipes. Provide with circulation pipe, etc., complete.

SINK.    Furnish and put up a 36 in. × 20 in. × 6 in. cast-iron sink, with iron legs, and supply it with hot and cold water, through ⅝-inch B supply pipes, ⅝-inch finished flange bibb cocks, 3-inch waste pipes and traps, and brass trap screw. Provide a copper branch and stop cock below the sink for emptying the boiler.

13

WASH-TRAYS.   Supply the two wash-trays in wash-room with hot and cold water through ⅝-inch strong B lead pipes, and ⅝-inch finished brass flange and thimble tray drawer cocks. Provide with strainers, plugs and chains, and overflow from one tray to connect with waste-pipe. Furnish 3-inch main lead waste-pipe, weighing 5 pounds per lineal foot, trapped and connected with soil pipe, with 2-inch branch wastes connected with each tray. Trays to be lined with zinc.

FURNACE.   Supply the furnace with cold water through ½-inch strong B lead pipe, a 24 in. × 24 in. × 12 in. cistern lined with 4½-pound lead, a 4-inch copper ball and ball-cock, and connect with the evaporator by a copper pipe.

WATER-CLOSET.   Furnish and set in 2d story, as per plans, a best constructed pan closet, with white marble pattern basin, Wedgewood ware, enameled receiver and silver plated cup and handle. Provide with 24 in. × 14 in. × 14 inch cistern lined with 4-pound lead, and furnished with box, valve wire, 5-inch copper ball and ball-cock, etc., complete. Make the closet trap of 6-pound sheet lead.

WASH-BASIN.   Furnish and put in complete, in the 2d story, as per plans, a 14½-inch very best marble pattern Wedgewood-ware basin, supplied with hot and cold water, through ½-inch strong B lead pipe, No. 3 silver-plated upright basin cocks, with the requisite strainers, plug, chain and overflow, plated as above. Provide with white Italian veined marble top and base; the base 12 inches high; countersink the top, and mould the edge of it and the base; furnish with ½-inch overflow pipe and 2½-inch trapped lead waste.

BATH.   Furnish and fit up in 2d story, as per plans, one 18-oz. sheet copper, tinned and planished bath, supplied with hot and cold water, through ⅝-inch strong B lead pipe, ⅝-inch silver-plated flange cocks, and waste through 1½-inch lead waste pipe, properly trapped, and supplied with silver-plated plug and chain. Provide with ½-inch overflow pipe and silver-plated strainer. Furnish and fit up over the tub an 8-inch copper rose shower, of the best pattern, tinned and planished. Supply with cold water through ½-inch strong B lead pipe and silver-plated stop-cock.

STOP-COCKS.    Provide and put in all necessary stop-cocks as required and directed. Properly trap and grade all the pipes.

ATTIC TANK.    Line the attic tank $5\frac{1}{2}$ ft. × 6 ft. × 3 feet deep throughout with $4\frac{1}{2}$-pound sheet lead, well spotted, tacked and soldered. Furnish with $3\frac{1}{2}$-inch lead overflow pipe, and connect with soil pipe to privy sink.

PUMP.    Furnish and fit up by the side of sink in wash-room, one of "Carr's" $35 combination lift and force pumps. Connect the same with cistern and well through $1\frac{1}{4}$-inch strong B lead pipes, provided with $2\frac{1}{4}$-inch stop-cocks, one on each pipe placed beneath the pump. Connect the pump with attic tank through 1-inch strong B lead pipe.

RANGE.    Furnish and set in kitchen fire-place one of the most approved Cooking Ranges of the largest size the space assigned will admit, and of the kind selected by the owner. Fit up with all the requisite appliances, water-back, etc., and complete the present provision for discharging the ashes into the pit below.

WORKMANSHIP, ETC.    All the work to be executed in the best and most thorough workman-like manner, and warranted perfect and substantial in operation at the completion. All the plated work to be of the best, first-class description, and the pipes and metal used to be *fully up to the standard called for.* This will be *rigidly enforced* by the Superintending Architect.

Any other required pipes or other work or materials, to supply, empty and connect the several works, to be furnished.

Upon a due and sufficient performance of the work a certificate will be furnished by the Architect.

Plate No. 5.

Design No. 2.

Engr & print by KORFF BROTHERS, 54 William St. N.Y.

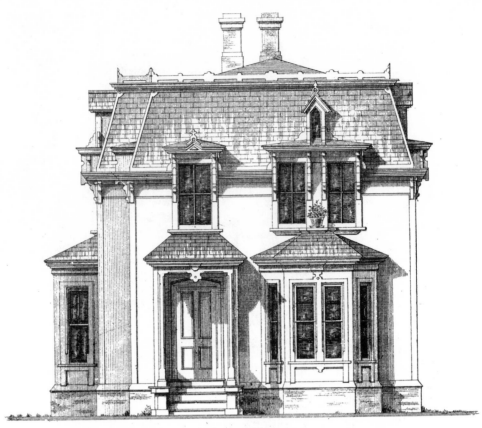

FRONT ELEVATION

SCALE. ⅛ Inch to One Foot.

SIDE ELEVATION.

SCALE. 1/16 Inch to One Foot.

Design No. 2.  Plate No. 7.

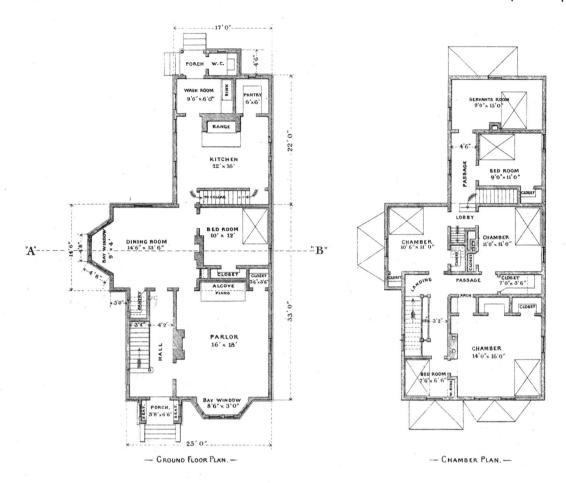

**Ground Floor Plan.**

17' 0"

PORCH  W.C.  4'6"

22' 0"

WASH ROOM
9'6" x 6'0"  SINK  PANTRY
6' x 6'

RANGE

KITCHEN
12' x 16'

TO CELLAR

BED ROOM
10' x 12'

"A"  DINING ROOM
14'6" x 13'6"  "B"

14'6"  BAY WINDOW
9' x 4'

4' 8"

CLOSET  CLOSET
3'6" x 3'6"

3' 0"  ALCOVE
PIANO

PANTRY

3' 4"  4' 2"

HALL

33' 0"

PARLOR
16' x 18'

SEAT  PORCH.  SEAT
3'8" x 6'6"

BAY WINDOW
8'6" x 3'0"

25' 0"

— Ground Floor Plan. —

**Chamber Plan.**

SERVANTS ROOM
9'0" x 15'0"

PASSAGE  4'6"

BED ROOM
9'0" x 11'0"  CLOSET

LOBBY

CHAMBER
10'6" x 11'0"  CHAMBER
11'0" x 11'0"

CLOSET  CLOSET

CLOSET

LANDING  PASSAGE  CLOSET
7'0" x 3'6"

3' 2"  ARCH  CLOSET

CHAMBER
14'0" x 16'0"

BED ROOM
7'6" x 6'6"  W. ROBE

— Chamber Plan. —

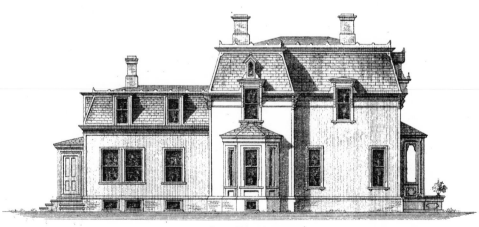

— Side Elevation. —

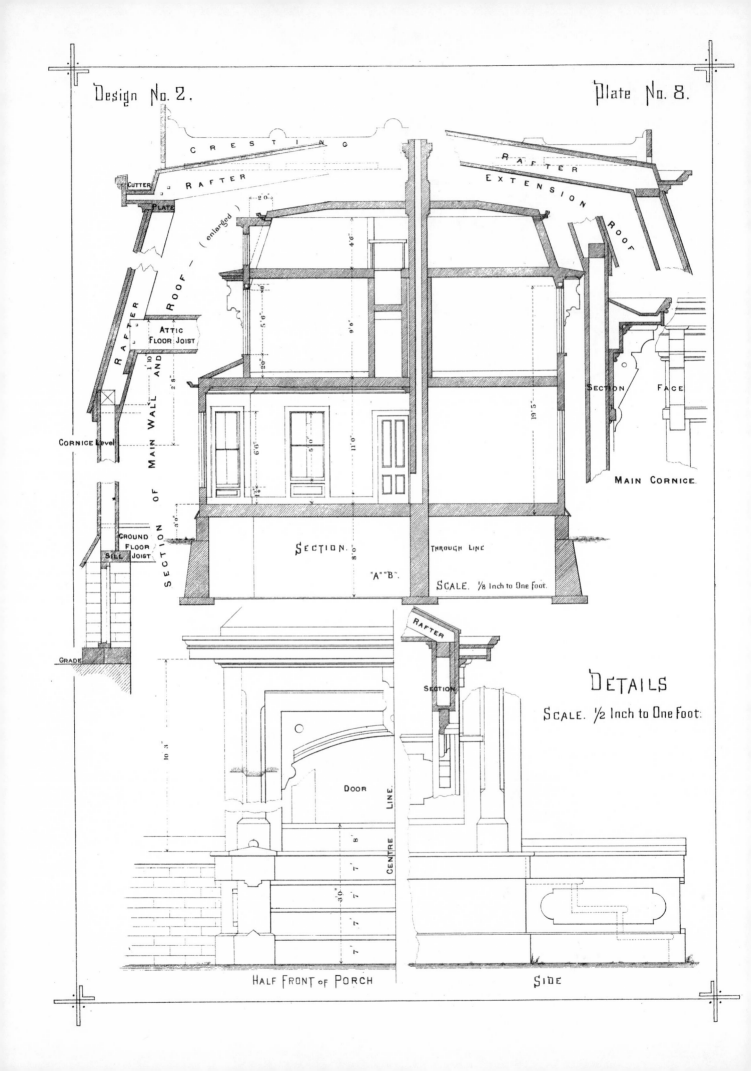

Design No. 2.                                        Plate No. 8.

CRESTING

RAFTER

CUTTER

PLATE

ROOF (enlarged)

RAFTER        EXTENSION        ROOF

RAFTER        ROOF

ATTIC
FLOOR JOIST

SECTION        FACE

CORNICE LEVEL

SECTION OF MAIN WALL AND

MAIN CORNICE.

GROUND
FLOOR JOIST

SILL

GRADE

SECTION.        THROUGH LINE

"A" "B".

SCALE. 1/8 Inch to One Foot.

RAFTER

SECTION

DETAILS

SCALE. 1/2 Inch to One Foot.

DOOR

CENTRE LINE.

HALF FRONT OF PORCH                    SIDE

Design No. 2.

Plate No. 9.

CENTRE LINE

CENTRE LINE

CENTRE LINE

DETAILS

OF

FRONT BAY WINDOW, DORMER &C

SCALE. ½ Inch to One Foot.

3' 0"

3' 8½"

1 8½"

6"

6"

6"

6"

6"

1 8½"

3½"

3' 0"

6"

Engr.& print by KORFF BROTHERS 54 William St. N.Y.

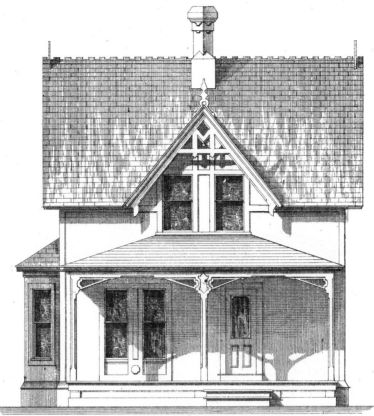

— FRONT ELEVATION. —

— SIDE ELEVATION. —

SCALE. ⅛ Inch to One Foot.

Engr & print by KORFF BROTHERS 54 William St. N.Y.

FRONT ELEVATION.
SCALE. ⅛ Inch to One Foot.

SIDE ELEVATION.
SCALE. ⅟₁₆ Inch to One Foot.

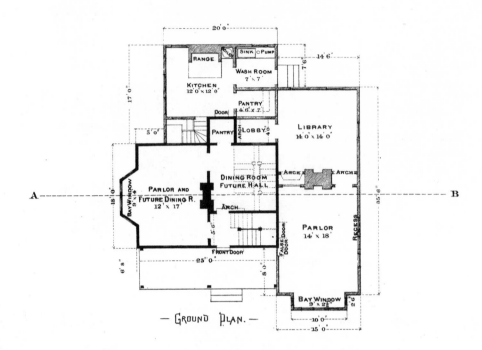

— Ground Plan. —

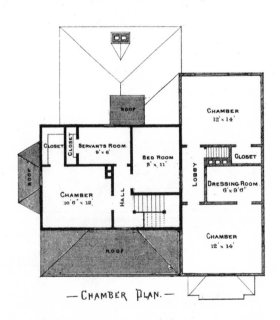

— Chamber Plan. —

Scale. 1/16 Inch to One Foot.

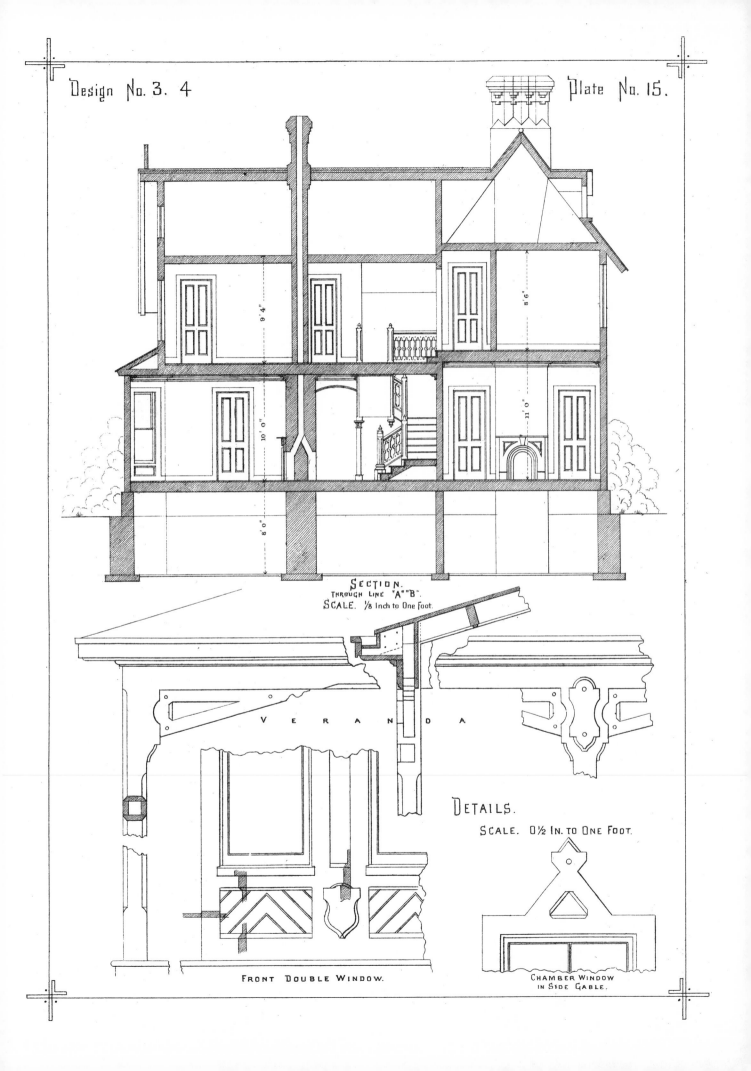

Design No. 3. 4

Plate No. 15.

9' 4"

8' 6"

10' 0"

11' 0"

8' 0"

SECTION.
THROUGH LINE "A" "B".
SCALE. 1/8 Inch to One Foot.

V E R A N D A

DETAILS.

SCALE. 0 1/2 In. to One Foot.

FRONT DOUBLE WINDOW.

CHAMBER WINDOW
IN SIDE GABLE.

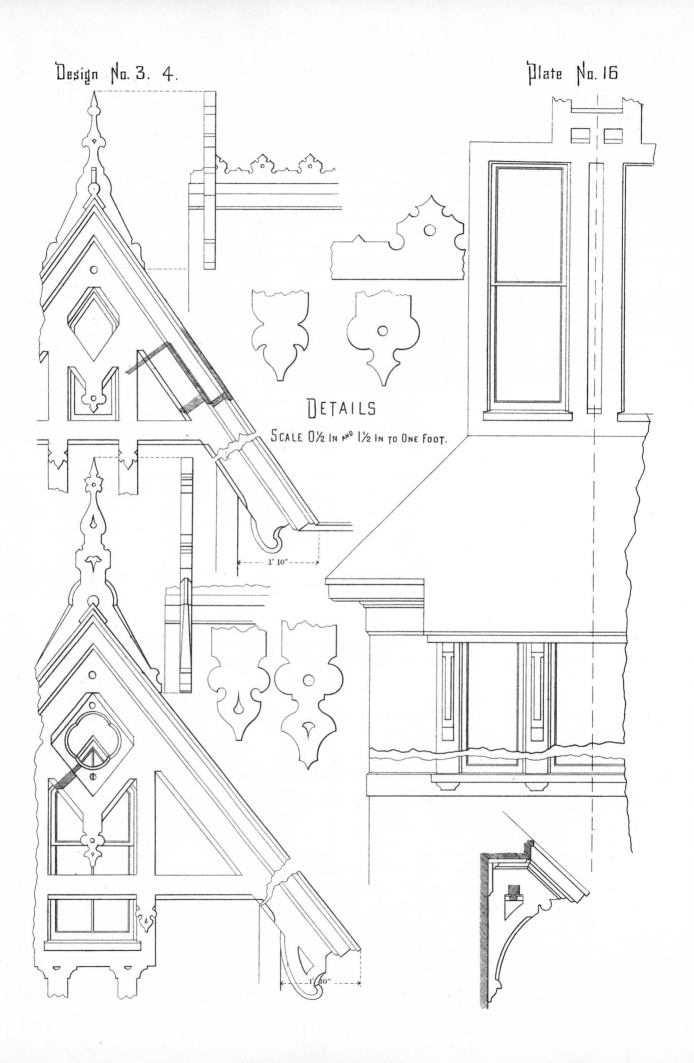

Design No. 3. 4.

Plate No. 16

DETAILS

SCALE 0½ IN AND 1½ IN TO ONE FOOT.

1' 10"

1' 10"

Design No. 5.

Plate No. 17.

Engr & print by KORFF BROTHERS 54 William St. N.Y.

FRONT ELEVATION
SCALE. 1/8 Inch to One foot.

SIDE ELEVATION.
SCALE. 1/16 Inch to One foot.

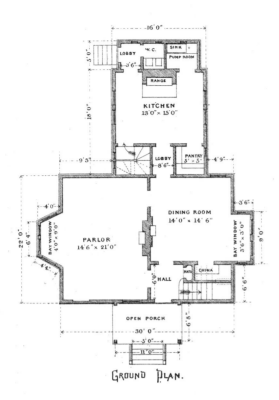

Ground Plan.

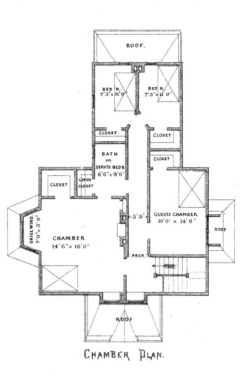

Chamber Plan.

Side Elevation.

SCALE. ¹⁄₁₆ Inch to One Foot.

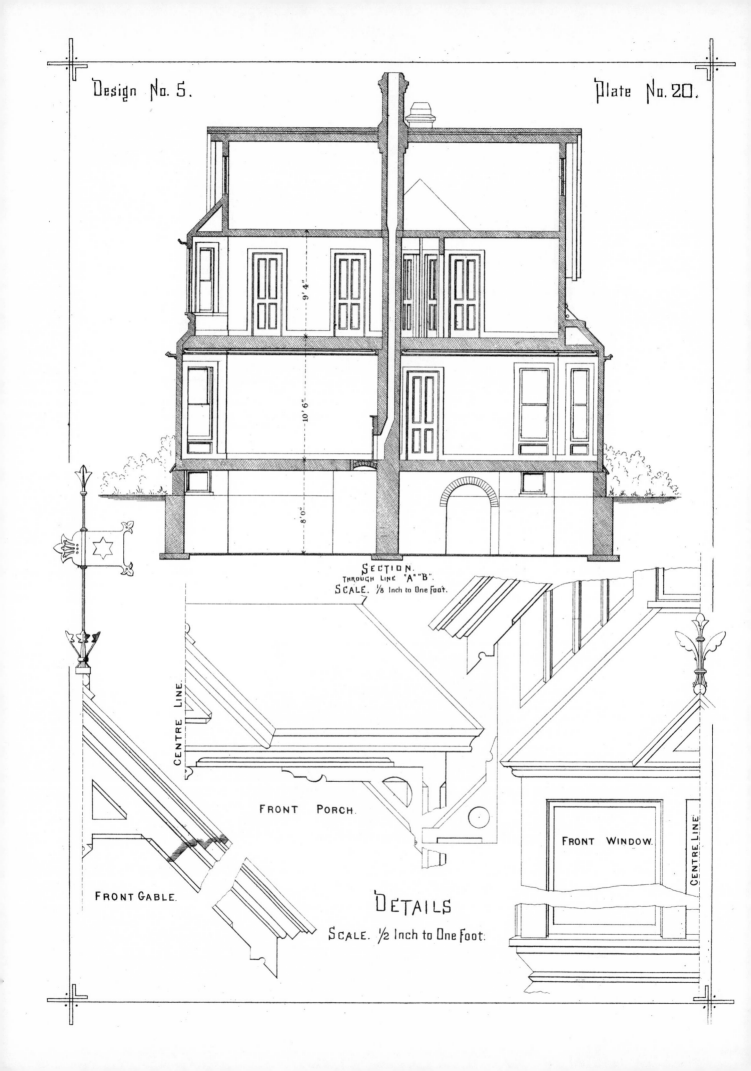

SECTION.
THROUGH LINE "A" "B".
SCALE. ⅛ Inch to One Foot.

9' 4"

10' 6"

8' 0"

CENTRE LINE.

FRONT PORCH.

FRONT GABLE.

FRONT WINDOW.

CENTRE LINE.

DETAILS

SCALE. ½ Inch to One Foot.

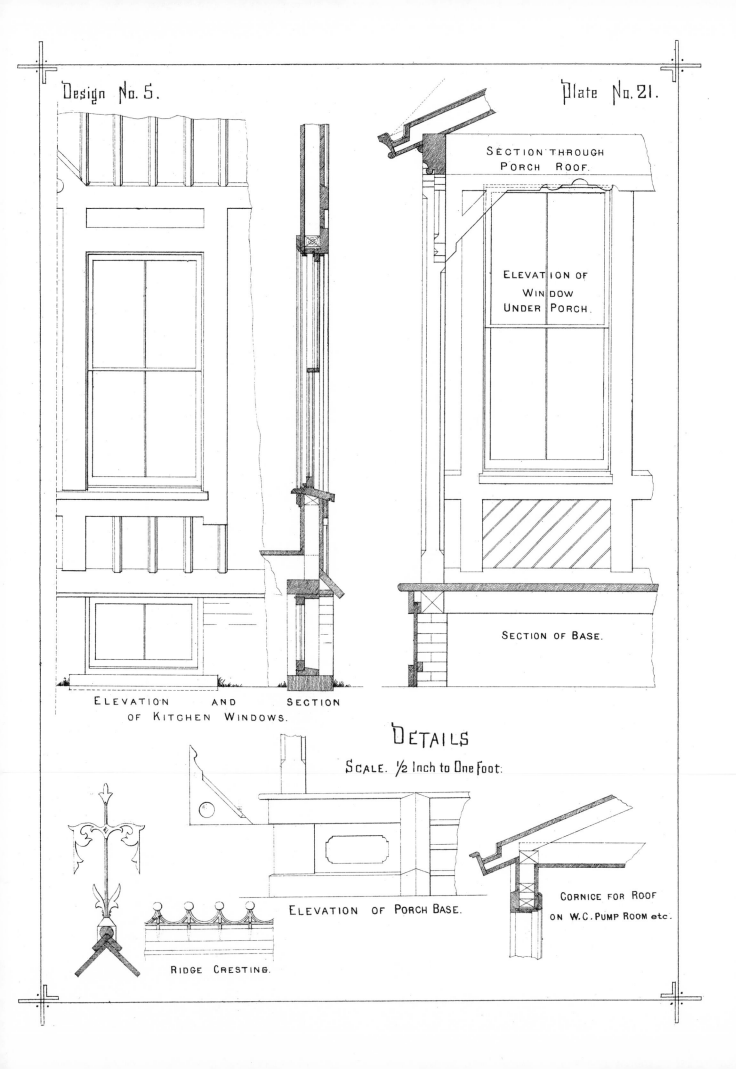

Design No. 5.

Plate No. 21.

SECTION THROUGH
PORCH ROOF.

ELEVATION OF
WINDOW
UNDER PORCH.

SECTION OF BASE.

ELEVATION AND SECTION
OF KITCHEN WINDOWS.

DETAILS

SCALE. ½ Inch to One Foot.

ELEVATION OF PORCH BASE.

CORNICE FOR ROOF
ON W.C. PUMP ROOM etc.

RIDGE CRESTING.

Eng'r & print by KORFF BROTHERS 54 William St. N.Y.

FRONT ELEVATION.

SCALE. 1/8 Inch to One Foot.

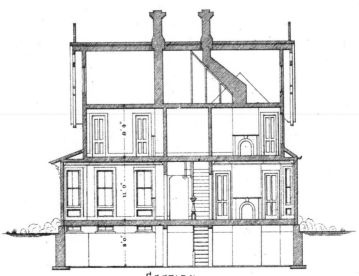

SECTION.
THROUGH LINE "A" "B".
SCALE. 1/16 Inch to One Foot.

Design No. 6

SIDE ELEVATION.

SCALE. 1/8 Inch to One Foot.

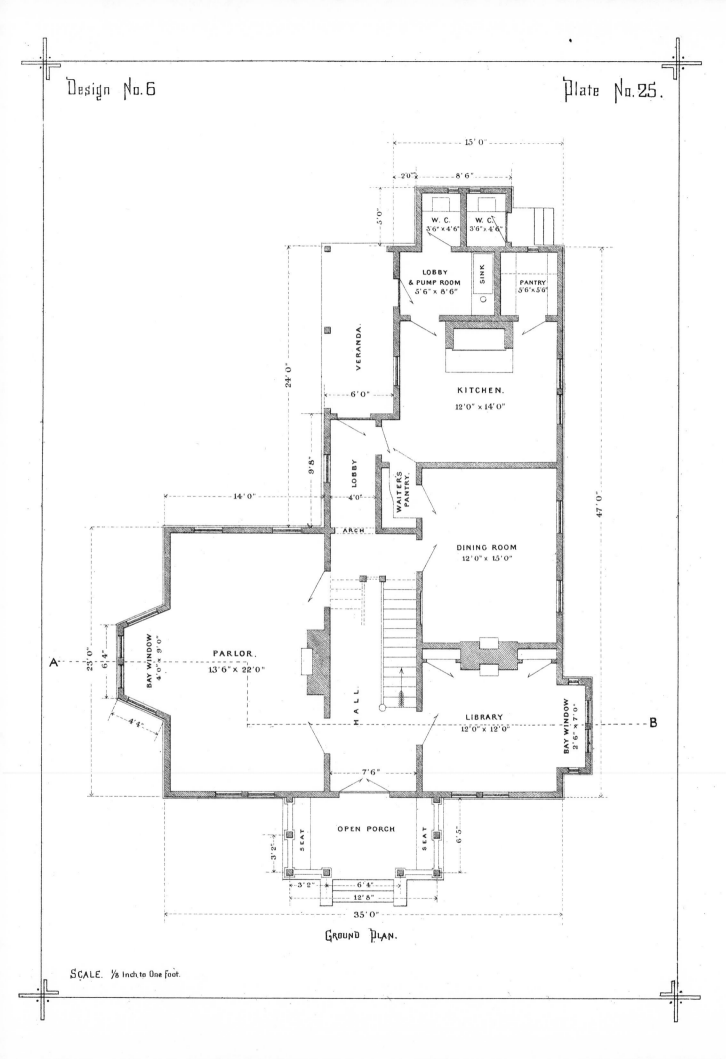

Design No. 6                                    Plate No. 25.

15' 0"

2' 0" x        8' 6"

5' 0"

W. C.          W. C.
3'6" x 4'6"    3'6" x 4'6"

LOBBY
& PUMP ROOM        SINK        PANTRY
5'6" x 8'6"                     5'6" x 5'6"

VERANDA.

24' 0"

KITCHEN.
12'0" x 14'0"

6' 0"

9' 8"

47' 0"

LOBBY

WAITER'S
PANTRY.

14' 0"          4'0"

ARCH

DINING ROOM
12'0" x 15'0"

23' 0"

BAY WINDOW
4'0" x 9'0"

6'4"

PARLOR.
13'6" x 22'0"

A

HALL

4' 4"

LIBRARY
12'0" x 12'0"

BAY WINDOW
2'6" x 7'0"

B

7'6"

OPEN PORCH

SEAT                SEAT

3' 2"                            6' 5"

3' 2"        6' 4"

12' 8"

35' 0"

GROUND PLAN.

SCALE. 1/8 Inch to One Foot.

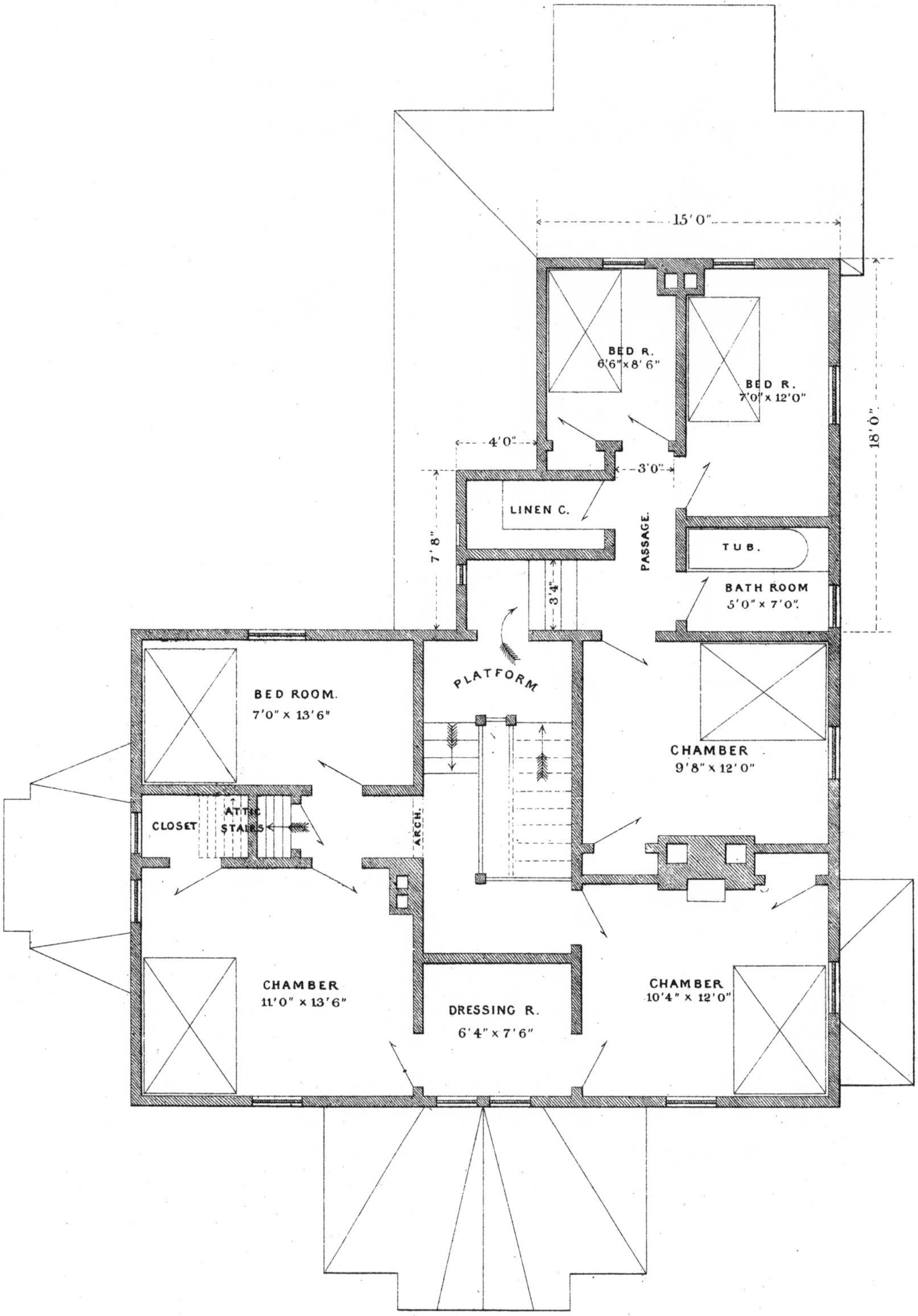

15'0"

18'0"

BED R.
6'6"x8'6"

BED R.
7'0" x 12'0"

4'0"

3'0"

7'8"

LINEN C.

PASSAGE.

TUB.

3'4"

BATH ROOM
5'0" x 7'0".

BED ROOM.
7'0" x 13'6"

PLATFORM

CHAMBER
9'8" x 12'0"

CLOSET

ATTIC
STAIRS

ARCH.

CHAMBER
11'0" x 13'6"

DRESSING R.
6'4" x 7'6"

CHAMBER
10'4" x 12'0"

CHAMBER PLAN.

SCALE. 1/8 Inch to One Foot.

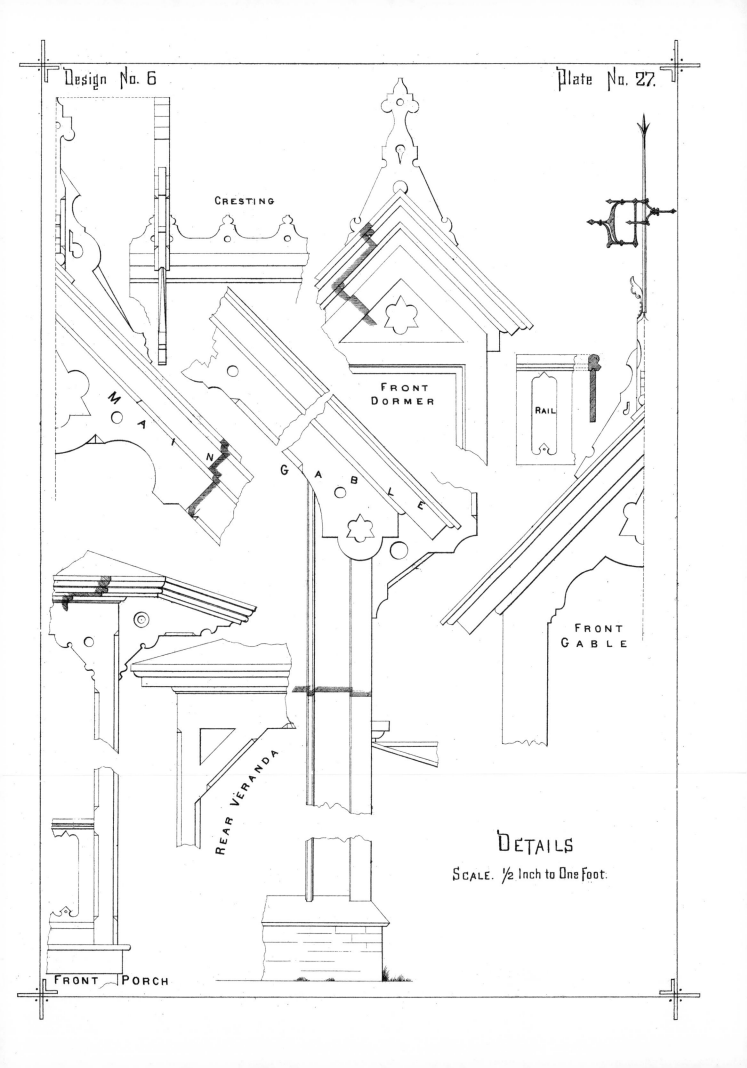

CRESTING

MAIN GABLE

FRONT DORMER

RAIL

FRONT GABLE

REAR VERANDA

FRONT PORCH

DETAILS

SCALE. ½ Inch to One Foot.

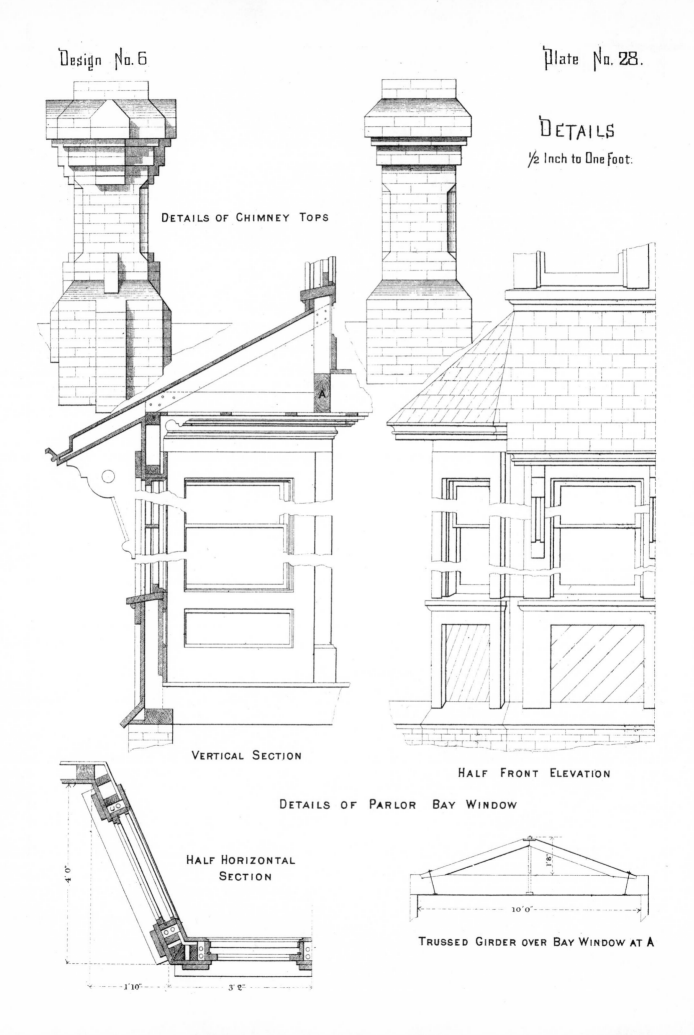

Design No. 6

Plate No. 28.

DETAILS OF CHIMNEY TOPS

DETAILS

½ Inch to One Foot:

A

VERTICAL SECTION

HALF FRONT ELEVATION

DETAILS OF PARLOR BAY WINDOW

HALF HORIZONTAL
SECTION

4' 0"

1' 10"          3' 2"

18"

10' 0"

TRUSSED GIRDER OVER BAY WINDOW AT A

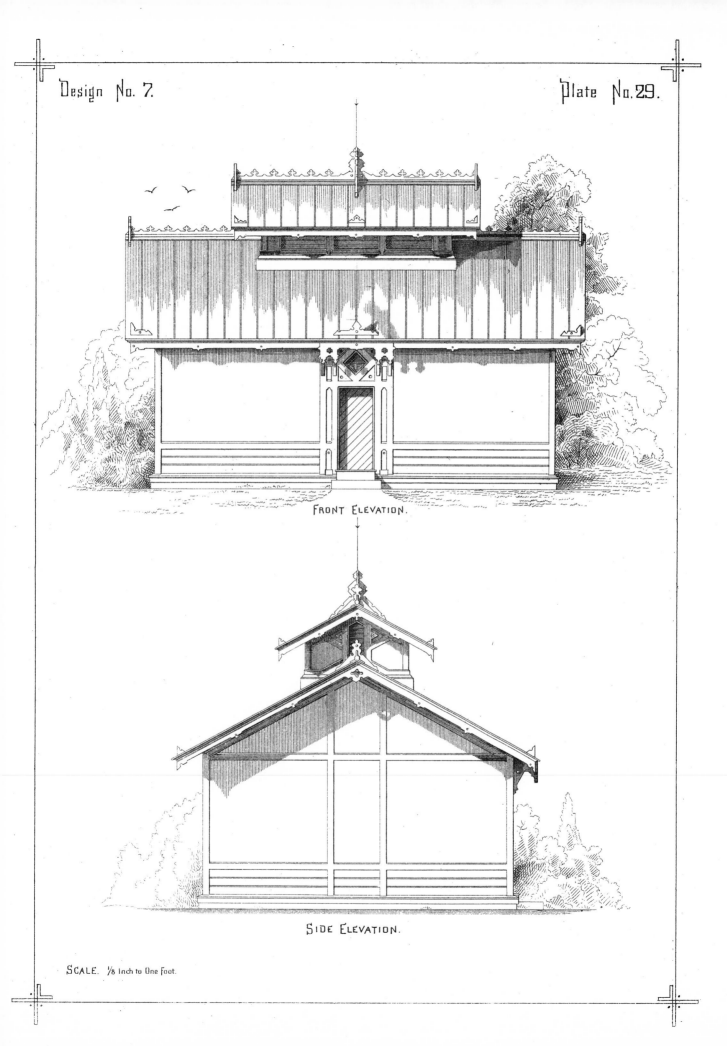

FRONT ELEVATION.

SIDE ELEVATION.

SCALE. 1/8 Inch to One Foot.

Design No. 7.                                                    Plate No. 30.

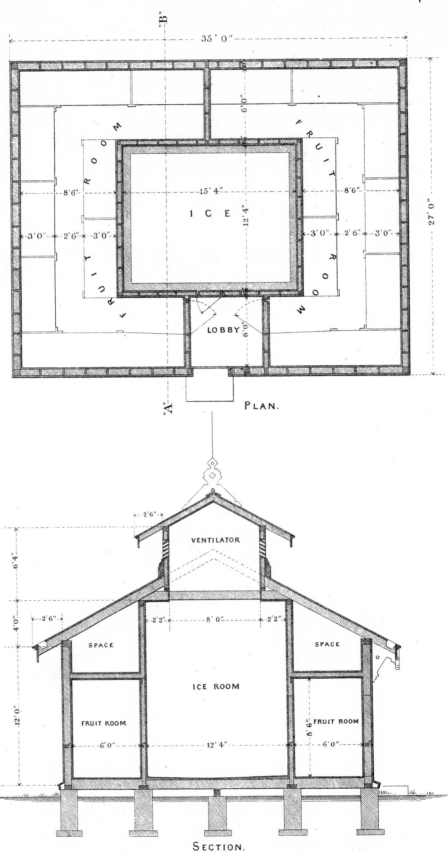

PLAN.

SECTION.
THROUGH LINE "A" "B"

SCALE. ⅛ Inch to One Foot.

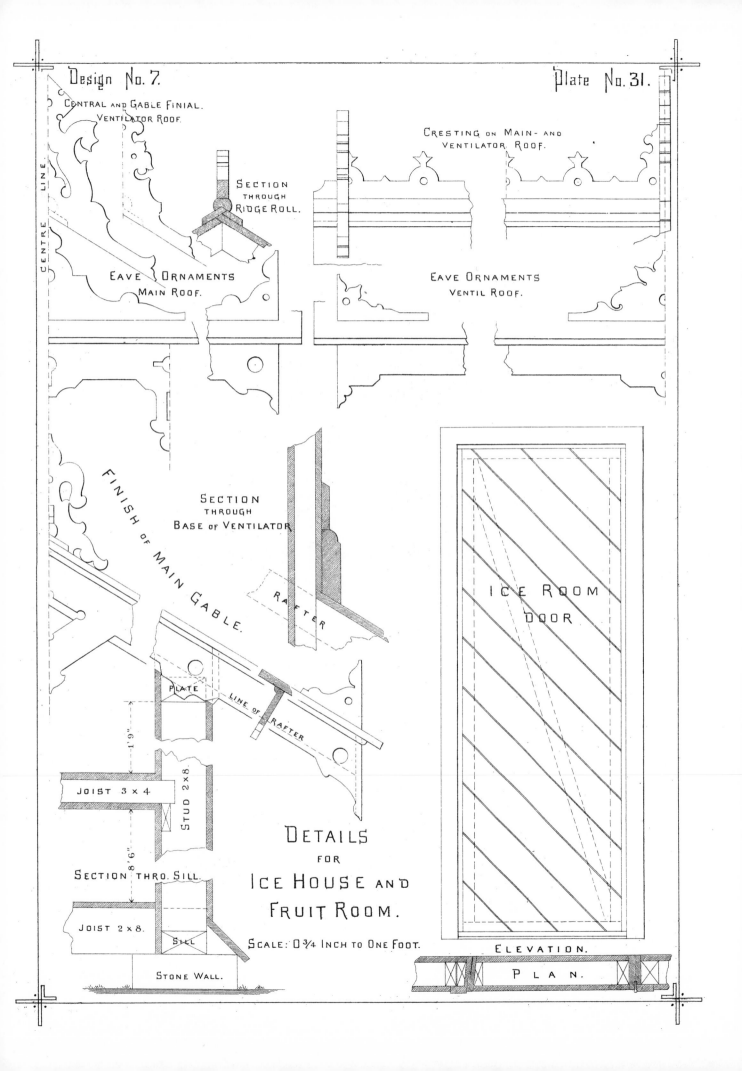

Design No. 7.                                                    Plate No. 31.

CENTRAL AND GABLE FINIAL.
VENTILATOR ROOF.

CENTRE LINE.

SECTION
THROUGH
RIDGE ROLL.

CRESTING ON MAIN- AND
VENTILATOR ROOF.

EAVE ORNAMENTS
MAIN ROOF.

EAVE ORNAMENTS
VENTIL ROOF.

FINISH OF MAIN GABLE.

SECTION
THROUGH
BASE OF VENTILATOR

RAFTER

PLATE

LINE OF RAFTER

1'9"

JOIST 3 × 4

STUD 2 × 8.

8'6"

SECTION THRO. SILL.

JOIST 2 × 8.

SILL.

STONE WALL.

ICE ROOM
DOOR

DETAILS
FOR
ICE HOUSE AND
FRUIT ROOM.

SCALE: 0¾ INCH TO ONE FOOT.

ELEVATION.

PLAN.

Design No. 8.                    Plate No. 32.

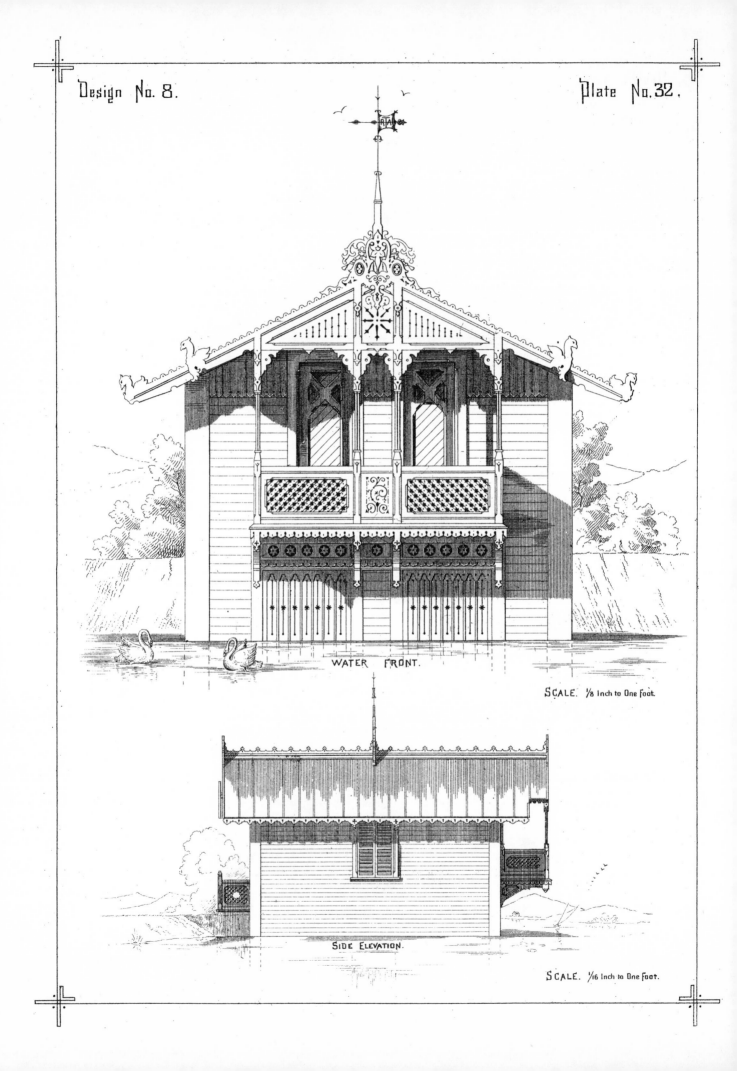

WATER FRONT.

SCALE. 1/8 Inch to One Foot.

SIDE ELEVATION.

SCALE. 1/16 Inch to One Foot.

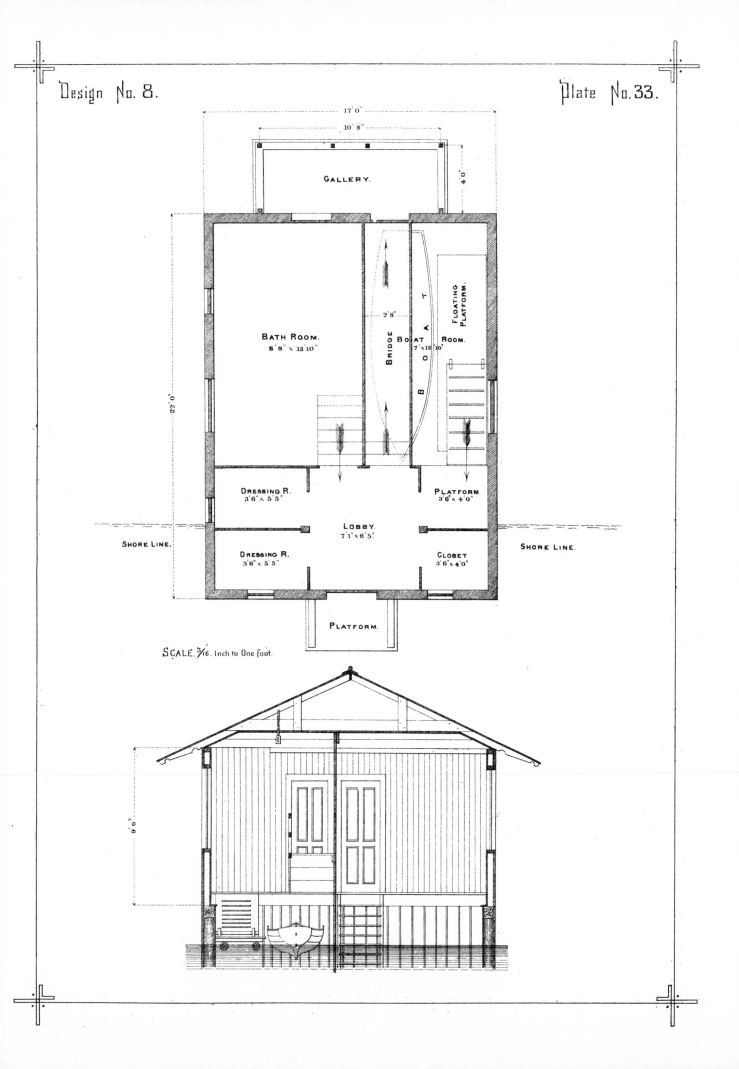

17' 0"

10' 8"

GALLERY.

4' 0"

22' 0"

BATH ROOM.
8' 8" x 13' 10"

2' 8"

BRIDGE

BOAT ROOM.
7' x 13' 10"

FLOATING PLATFORM.

DRESSING R.
3' 6" x 5' 5"

PLATFORM
3' 6" x 4' 0"

LOBBY.
7' 1" x 6' 5"

SHORE LINE.

SHORE LINE.

DRESSING R.
3' 6" x 5' 5"

CLOSET
3' 6" x 4' 0"

PLATFORM.

SCALE. 3/16. Inch to One Foot.

9' 0"

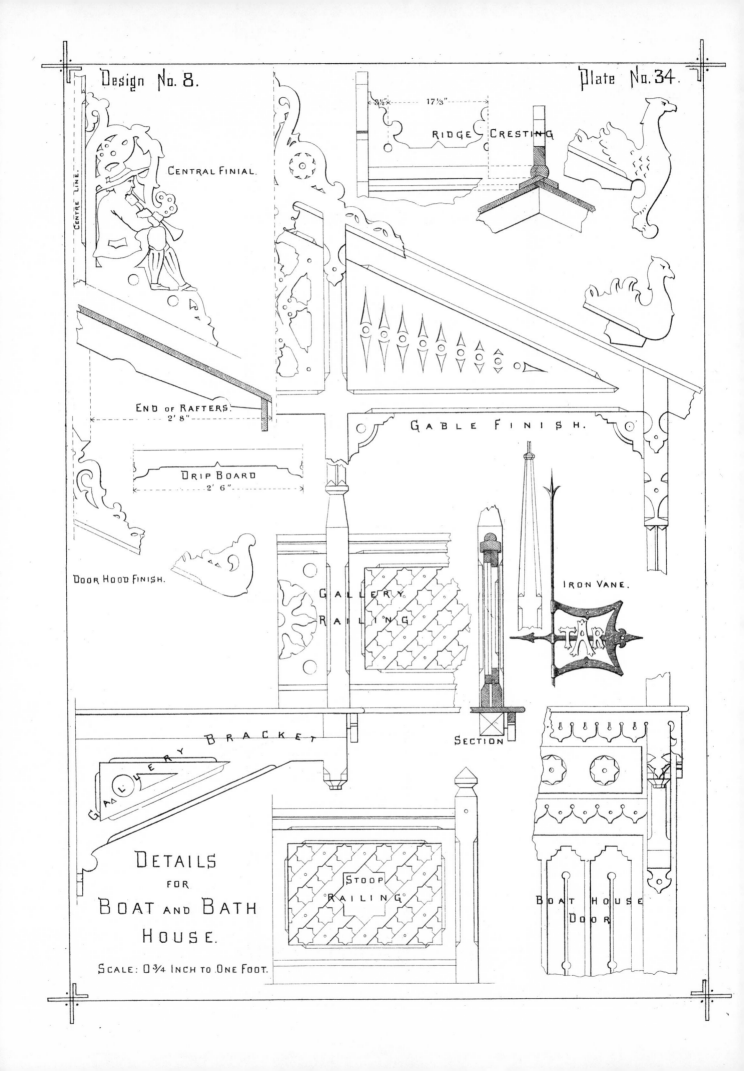

Design No. 8.

Plate No. 34.

Central Finial.

Ridge Cresting.

17⅓"

3½"

End of Rafters 2'8"

Gable Finish.

Drip Board 2' 6"

Door Hood Finish.

Gallery Railing.

Iron Vane.

T.A.R.

Section.

Gallery Bracket.

Stoop Railing.

Boat House Door.

Details for Boat and Bath House.

Scale: 0 ¾ Inch to One Foot.

Centre Line.

Engr & print by KORFF BROTHERS 54 William St N.Y.

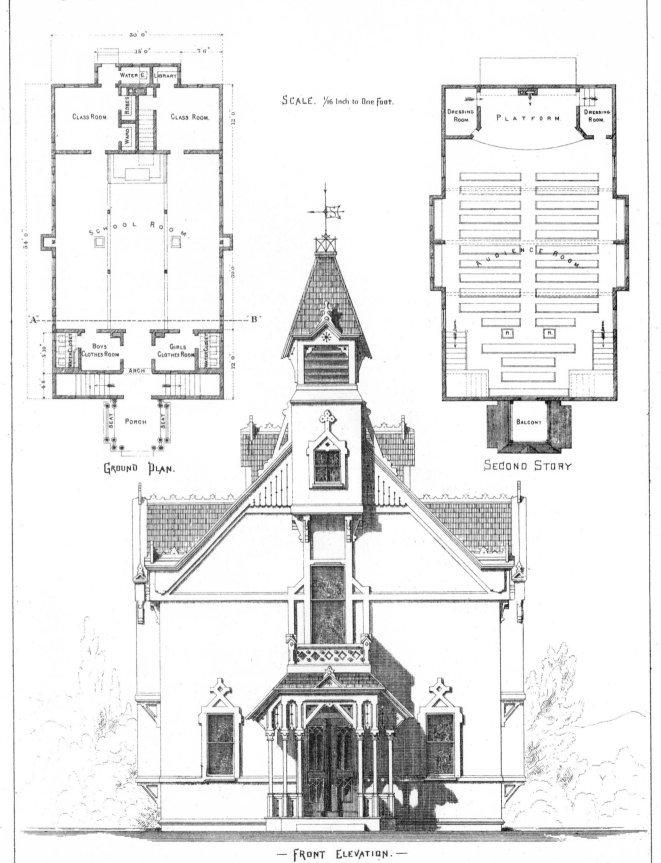

30' 0"
15' 0"          7' 6"

WATER C. | LIBRARY

CLASS ROOM.        WARD ROBES        CLASS ROOM.

12' 0"

SCHOOL ROOM.

30' 0"

54' 0"

A"                                    B"

5' 10"

WATER CLOSET | BOYS CLOTHES ROOM        GIRLS CLOTHES ROOM | WATER CLOSET

12' 0"

ARCH

4' 8"

SEAT        PORCH        SEAT

GROUND PLAN.

SCALE. 1/16 Inch to One Foot.

DRESSING ROOM        PLATFORM        DRESSING ROOM

A U D I E N C E   R O O M

R.        R.

BALCONY

SECOND STORY

— FRONT ELEVATION. —

SCALE. 1/8 Inch to One Foot.

Design No. 9.

Side Elevation.

Scale. 1/8 Inch to One Foot.

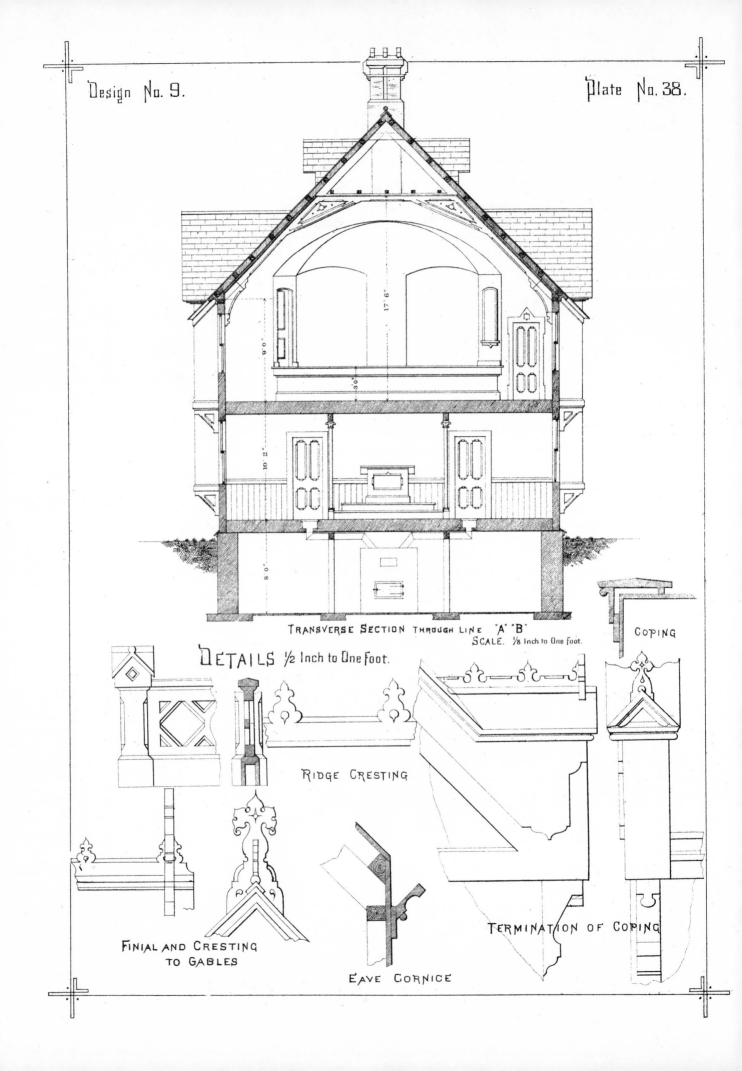

Design No. 9.

Plate No. 38.

17' 6"

9' 0"

3' 0"

10' 2"

8' 0"

TRANSVERSE SECTION THROUGH LINE "A" "B"
SCALE. 1/8 Inch to One Foot.

DETAILS 1/2 Inch to One Foot.

COPING

RIDGE CRESTING

FINIAL AND CRESTING
TO GABLES

EAVE CORNICE

TERMINATION OF COPING

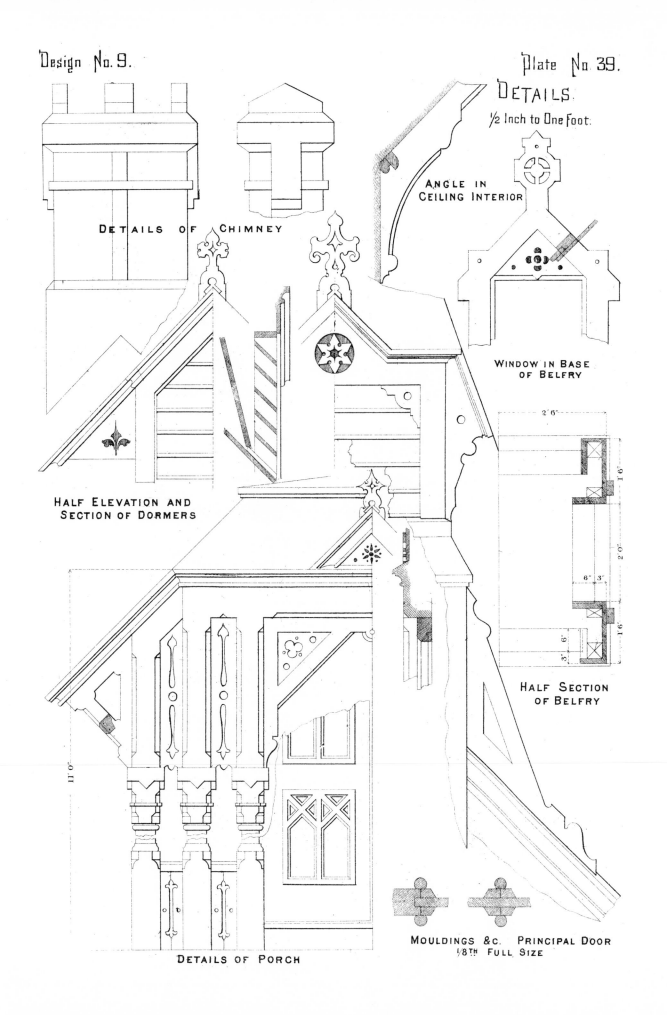

Design No. 9.

Plate No. 39.

DETAILS.

½ Inch to One Foot.

DETAILS OF CHIMNEY

ANGLE IN
CEILING INTERIOR

WINDOW IN BASE
OF BELFRY

HALF ELEVATION AND
SECTION OF DORMERS

2' 6"

1' 6"

2' 0"

6" 3"

1' 6"

3" 6"

HALF SECTION
OF BELFRY

11' 0"

DETAILS OF PORCH

MOULDINGS &c. PRINCIPAL DOOR
1/8TH FULL SIZE

Plate No. 40.

Design No. 10

Engr & print by KORFF BROTHERS 54 William St. N.Y.

Design No. 10

FRONT ELEVATION.

SCALE. ⅛ Inch to One foot.

Design No. 10

SIDE ELEVATION.

SCALE. 1/8 Inch to One foot.

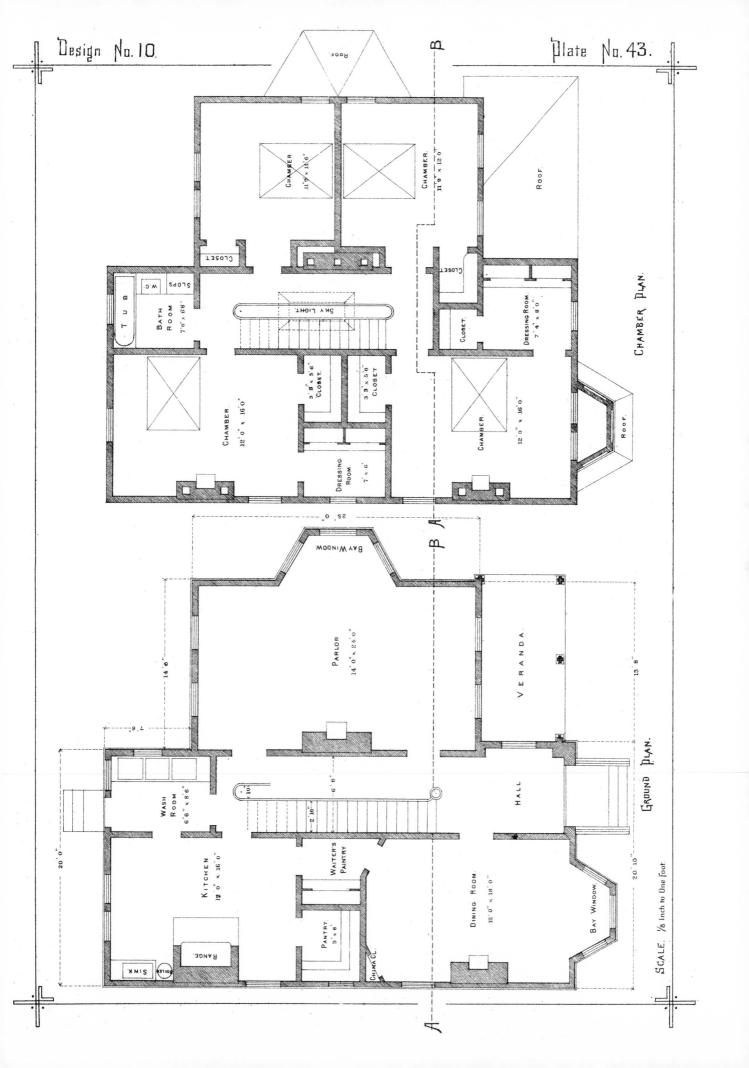

Design No. 10.

Plate No. 43.

CHAMBER PLAN.

CHAMBER
11'9" x 11'6"

CHAMBER
11'9" x 12'0"

ROOF.

CLOSET

W.C.  SLOPS

TUB

BATH ROOM
7'0" x 6'6"

CLOSET

CLOSET.

DRESSING ROOM
7'4" x 8'0"

ROOF.

SKY LIGHT

3'8" x 5'6"
CLOSET.

3'3" x 5'6"
CLOSET

CHAMBER
12'0" x 16'0"

CHAMBER
12'0" x 16'0"

DRESSING ROOM
7' x 6'

25'0"

14'6"

BAY WINDOW.

PARLOR
14'0" x 24'0"

VERANDA.

7'6"

6'6"

2'10"

1'10"

WASH ROOM
6'6" x 8'6"

HALL

13'8"

20'0"

KITCHEN
12'0" x 16'0"

WAITER'S PANTRY

PANTRY
5' x 6'

CHINA CL.

DINING ROOM
12'0" x 18'0"

BAY WINDOW

RANGE.

SINK

BOILER

20'10"

GROUND PLAN.

SCALE. 1/8 Inch to One Foot.

A

B

B

A

SECTION.
THROUGH LINE "A" "B"
SCALE. ⅛ Feet to One Inch

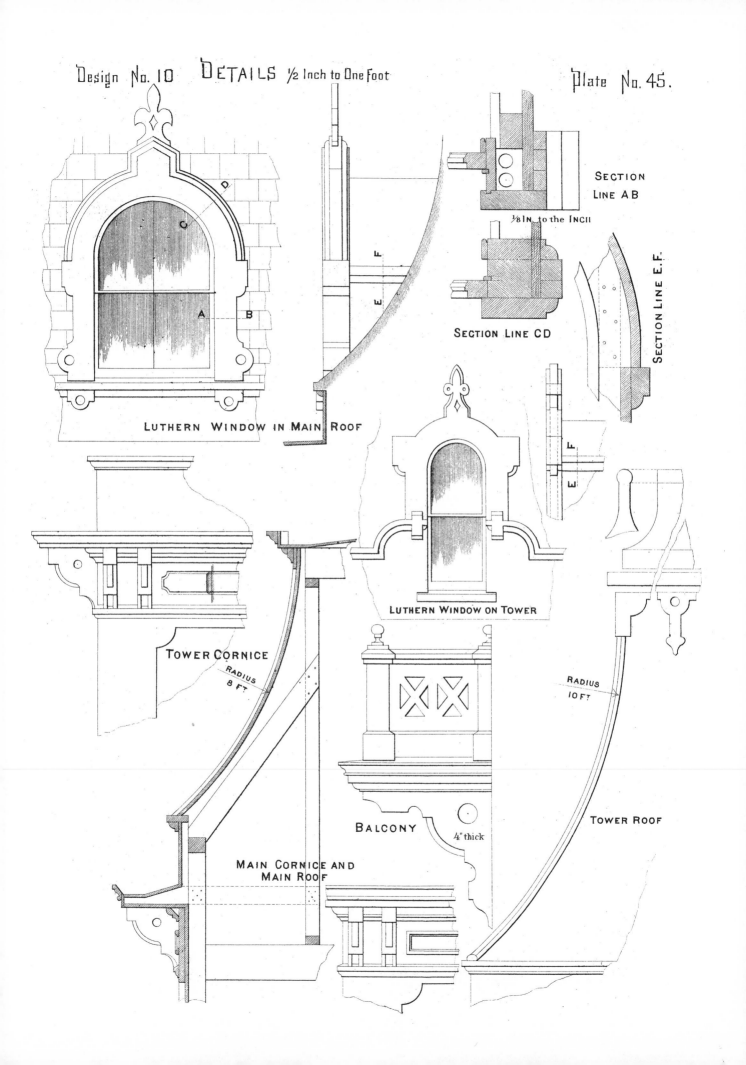

LUTHERN WINDOW IN MAIN ROOF

SECTION LINE A B

⅛ IN. to the INCH

SECTION LINE CD

SECTION LINE E.F.

LUTHERN WINDOW ON TOWER

TOWER CORNICE

RADIUS 8 FT

RADIUS 10 FT

BALCONY

4" thick

TOWER ROOF

MAIN CORNICE AND MAIN ROOF

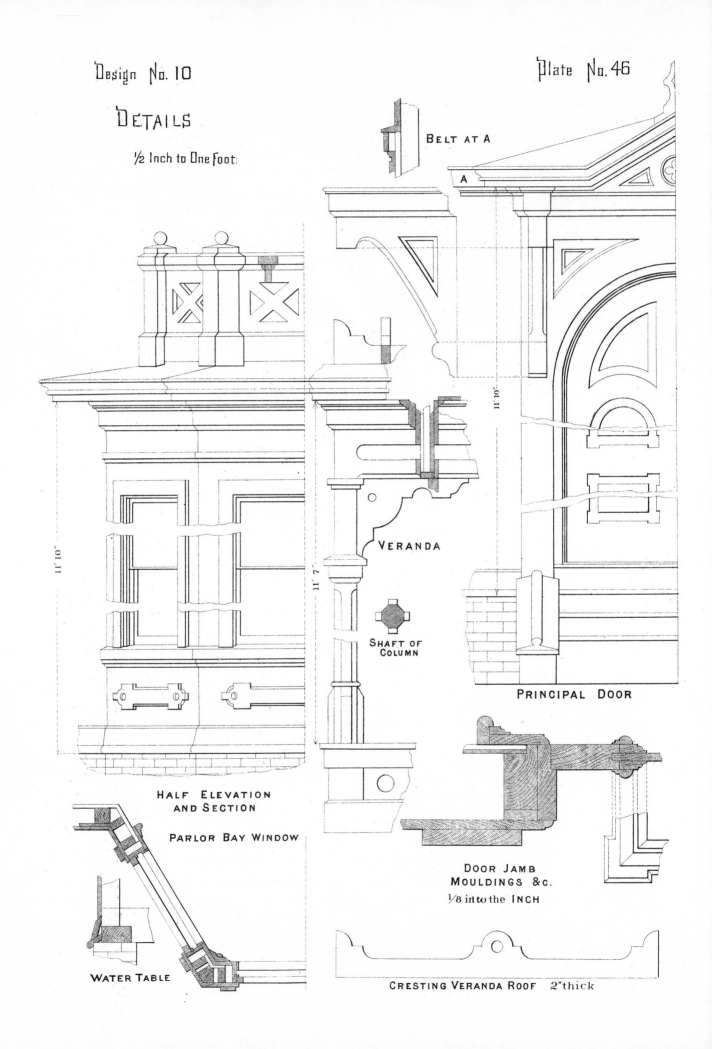

Design No. 10

DETAILS

½ Inch to One Foot.

Plate No. 46

BELT AT A

A

VERANDA

SHAFT OF
COLUMN

PRINCIPAL DOOR

HALF ELEVATION
AND SECTION

PARLOR BAY WINDOW

WATER TABLE

DOOR JAMB
MOULDINGS &c.
⅛ in to the INCH

CRESTING VERANDA ROOF 2" thick

# DESIGN No. 10.

# CARPENTERS' SPECIFICATION.

———————▶◀·◆·▶◀———————

DIMENSIONS.　　　　General dimensions, height of stories, and internal arrangement to be obtained from the drawings.

MATERIALS.　　　　Furnish all the materials the best of their several kinds ; the lumber of white pine when not otherwise specified, well-seasoned and dry.

Sashes and panel work in all cases to be of perfectly clear lumber.

## TIMBERING.

Furnish the following timber of white pine.

Sills, 4×8 inches, laid on the flat and halved together at the angles.

Angle-posts, 4×6 inches. Intermediate posts 4×4 inches, spiked to the sills.

Girts (first one above the sills), 4×4 inches, spiked to the posts and studs.

2d Girt (above sills), 7×1 inch gained into the studs and posts.

Wall and steep roof plates 4×4 inches.

Girders in cellar, 5×5 inches.

1st and 3d tier of beams, 9×2 inches.　16 inches from centres.

2d tier of beams, 10×2 inches.　　　　　"　　　　　"

Steep pitch rafters, 2×6 inches.　　　　"　　　　　"

Flat rafters and tie beams or ceiling joist, 8×2.　2 feet from centres.

Hip and valley rafters, 9×3 inches.

Carriage beams and headers 4 inches thick.

Ridge plates of flat roofs, 9 × 1 inch.

Also furnish the following of Hemlock :

Nailing joist (through 1st story), 5 × 2 inches.   16 inches from centres.

    "   "  (above   "  ) 4 × 2  "       "         "

Braces (long,) 4 × 4 inches, nailed in barefoot.

    "  (short) 4 × 3  "    "    "

Studs supporting ridge plate, 4 × 2 inches.   16 inches from centres.

**BRIDGING.**

Cut in two rows of cross bridging in each tier of beams.

All the above timber to be perfectly sound, square-edged straight timber, free from all imperfections impairing its durability or strength.  Also, furnish, of like quality, timber for the

**PIAZZA**

of the following sizes:

Sills and cross sills (at each post), 4 × 6 inches.

Floor joist, 6 × 2 inches, 2 feet from centres.

Plates, 8 × 4 inches.   Rafters, 6 × 2 inches.

Furnish the required substantial frame for the front platform and steps.

Furnish any other timber required by the design of the requisite size and quality.

**FRAMING.**

Execute all the framing in the most thoroughly workmanlike manner, substantially and firmly spiked together in the style known as "Balloon" framing.

Double the floor beams under bearing partitions.

Supply and use anchors and anchoring strips if found requisite.

## EXTERIOR WORK.

**ROOFING**

Cover the Roofs with sound matched roofing boards, joints broken when practicable, and nail securely twice to each bearing.  Case up neatly the gutters as per drawings.

17

TINNING.    Cover the flat roof and dormers, and line the gutters with the best quality of charcoal roofing tin, the tin to extend well up into the brick-work of the chimney, and under and behind the siding with which it forms a joint. Convey the water from the gutters down to the grade level through the required number of XX tin leaders, firmly secured to the build-ing with galvanized iron holdfasts.

SLATING.    Cover the steep pitch roofs and the hood over front door with the best quality of purple slate, 16 in. long, laid 6½ in. to the weather.

Put zinc step flashings around the chimneys and dormers.

Case for a scuttle 2 × 3 feet in size in roof of flat where directed, and furnish with strong tongued plank cover, tinned, hung on butt hinges, and fastened with hook and staple.

Trim for a sky-light with 2-in. plank cheeks rebated to receive the sash.

Case up and mould the cresting surmounting tower, also the gutter cornice mould of flat roof and the hip angle boards, all as per detail and elevation drawings.

DORMERS, CORNI-    Build the dormer windows in all respects as shown by the scale and
CES, ETC.    detail drawings, also the moulded sill courses, cornices, balconies, bay win-dows, piazza posts, brackets and cornice, string and belt courses, front door hood, water-table, etc.

The piazza ceiling and soffit of the door hood to be sheathed with clear narrow-tongued and beaded sheathing. Floor the piazzas with narrow 1¼-inch tongued boards not over 3½ inches wide, in one length and blind nailed, with white lead joints. Build the platform and steps in front with 1¼-inch strings and treads, and 1-inch risers and enclosed facias, surmounted with moulded capping, all as per scale and detail drawings. Put cove moulding under the tread nosings. Enclose below piazza floor down to the grade with facia, base, scroll-sawed panels, etc.

Build plain steps to rear outside entrance, as shown.

The panels in frieze of main cornice to be formed with raised mouldings.

Case the windows and doors with plain casings, sawed in form as shown, 1¼-inch thick, surmounted with 2-inch coved head bands.

18

The panels of tower cornice and of bay windows will be raised 1¼ inch with moulded edges.

Furnish the cresting for piazza and bay window roofs, scroll-sawed from 1½-inch plank.

**SIDE SHEATH-ING.**

Sheath up all around the building with perfectly sound and nearly clear ⅞-inch boards.

To be as nearly 8 inches in width as will conform in courses to the top and bottom of window frames, etc., all tongued and rebated from the top of water-table to the belt course level with the piazza and bay window cornices.

Furnish the windows with 2½-inch rebated sills.

Sheath the sides of the building all around above the belt course with narrow tongued sheathing, not exceeding 4½-inch width, flush joints.

Form gutters in the piazza roof.

Furnish small scroll-sawed finials and corbels to tower windows, etc., as shown.

Furnish any other outside trimmings required by the design.

Floor over the tin roof of front bay window with narrow framed 1¼-in. slats, ½ inch apart, firred up clear from the tin roof.

## FLOORING.

Lay the attic floor with 8×1-inch sound tongued lumber, well nailed through the top.

Lay the 1st and 2d story floors with perfectly sound tongued boards 3½ to 4½×1-in, blind-nailed.

Flush off the joints of the floors throughout with the plane.

Cut in 2×½-in borders around all the hearths.

Put down hard-wood saddles to all the doors.

## PARTITIONS AND FIRRING.

Cross fir the 1st story ceiling with 2×1-inch strips, 12 inches from centres.

19

Firr down the closet ceilings to a clear height of eight feet.

Cross firr the attic ceiling with 2 × 1-inch strips, 16 inches from centres.

Firr off the small rectangular dome over stairway, as shown by the plans and detail drawings.

Firr out from the steep pitch rafters to form the curved slope of the roof, with 1½-inch plank, sawed to the required form, also for the main cornices, as shown.

Do any other firring that the design requires.

Set all the partitions that support beams with 2 × 4-inch hemlock, 12 inches from centres, with 4 × 3-inch plates (square-edged, straight and sound) and 4 × 3-inch sills. Set all other partitions with 4 × 2-inch hemlock, 16 inches from centres. Set up the necessary studs and plates from ceiling joist in attic to support flat rafters.

Bridge all the partitions once in their height.

Form all the angles in partitions solid, and set the door studs double.

Set grounds to all openings and leave on.

CRESTING.

Provide the steep roof ridge with iron cresting as per elevation. Also furnish the iron finials and crestings on tower roof.


## STAIRS.

Build the cellar flight of stairs with 1½-inch strings and 1¼-inch treads, planed up and grooved together. Provide with pine slat rail through the cellar, and enclose in the 1st story with plastered partition, with door at the head.

Build the principal flight of stairs, extending from first story to attic, with 1¼-inch strings and treads, and 1-inch risers and facias, the steps front and back tongued. Mould the nosings and the front string.

Mould the wall string on top to correspond with the base in the hall.

Support the whole on 7 × 2-inch timbers, rough bracketed to each tread.

Surmount the whole with 3 × 4½-inch compound moulded rail, 2-inch fancy turned balusters, and supply an 8-inch octagon veneered newel at the start. The rail, balusters and newel to be of black walnut, well rubbed down with oil, and finished with shellac.

Plane up and groove together a neat step ladder to the scuttle.


## WINDOWS AND GLAZING.

Make the cellar window frames with two 2-inch plank, rebated for the sash. The sash to be 1½-inch thick, hinged at the top, and be fastened up and down with iron buttons.

Make the two small frames in rear of attic hall in a similar manner, with sash hung on hinges to open sideways; fasten as above described.

Make the attic front windows and the front parlor windows for hinging the lower casement, in the French manner—the upper to be hung,

All the windows, not otherwise above specified, to be provided with the usual box frames, and double hung sash, with 2-inch patent axle pulleys and best hemp cord. All the sash, except attic and cellar, to be 1¾-inch thick, and all to be made in the best manner, with weather lipped meeting rails. All other window sash throughout to be 1½-inch thick.

Glaze all the windows with the best quality of English sheet glass.

Style of sash, number of lights, etc., to be as shown upon the drawings.

Furnish an hipped sky-light of the best water-tight construction, placed over the dome. Glaze with corrugated glass.

Fasten all the window sash with the most approved style of sash fastenings, corresponding in finish with the neighboring door and bell furniture.


## DOORS, Etc.

Make the front doors 2¼-inch thick, paneled as per elevation and detail drawings, with raised mouldings.

Glaze the centre panels with the best quality of enameled glass of such pattern as the owner may select.

Make the first story principal room doors 1¾-inch thick and six panels each, and all other room doors 1½-inch thick and four panels each, all to be faced with mouldings.

Make the door opening from main hall to wash-room a sash-door, glazed above with enameled glass, and paneled below to correspond with the neighboring solid doors.

HINGING.    Hang all the doors on butt hinges of the most approved manufacture and the required size.

LOCKS.    Fasten the cellar and attic doors with rim locks, and all other doors throughout with mortice locks of the best city manufacture. Extra size lock with night-latch apparatus, to be placed on the front door.

BOLTS.    Provide each outside door with strong malleable iron shove bolts, of appropriate finish; tail bolts for the double doors.

FURNITURE.    Bronze metallic furniture to be used throughout the principal rooms and hall of the first story, white porcelain in the second story, and dark mineral elsewhere throughout.

BELLS.    Fit up with copper wire in zinc tubes the following bells:
One pull from front door to kitchen.
One  "    "    parlor          "
One  "    "    dining-room     "
One  "    "    each chamber    "
One  "    "    one      "      in 2d story to servants' room in attic.
The furniture of the pulls to correspond with the neighboring door furniture.

## INSIDE FINISH.

Trim the doors and windows throughout the principal rooms and hall of first story with 6½-inch moulded and banded architraves, and put down 8½-in × 1½-inch moulded base.

Trim the second story throughout with 1-in moulded architraves, and put down 7-inch plain neck-moulded base. Elsewhere throughout trim with 4½-inch plain chamfered and beaded architraves, and (except in kitchen) put down 6-inch chamfered base.

Insert the foot of the base into ogee moulded carpet strips, rebated ½-inch to receive it.

Trim the windows in parlor and dining-room, and principal rooms in second story (including dressing-room), down to the floor with framed moulded and panel backs.

Trim all other windows throughout (above the cellar) with nosing sills and moulded aprons.

CUTTING, ETC.   Do all necessary cutting away for and repairing after the plumbers, gas-fitters, bell-hangers, hot-air workmen and others, and afford them all the usual facilities for the prosecution of their work. Screw down the floors over gas-pipes, etc.

BATH-ROOM.   Case up the bath-tub as per plan, and panel the front. Trim the wall over the tub with a neat surbase 8 inches in height.

Fit up the water-closet with 1¼-inch seats, riser, and brass hinged flap. Fit up the slop-basin in a similar manner. The fittings to be of black walnut throughout.

PANTRIES.   Fit up the kitchen and waiters' pantries as indicated on the plans, with shelves and dovetailed drawers. The shelves in waiters' pantry to be enclosed with panel doors fastened with cupboard locks, and all the drawers to have drawer locks.

WARDROBES, CLOSETS, ETC.   Fit up the dressing-rooms with wardrobes enclosed with panel doors, with low foot drawers below. The doors and drawers fastened as above.

Fit up the closets with top shelves as indicated on the plans, and in these and the wardrobes put up the required number of double iron clothes hooks.

The shelves and hooks to be put up on neat moulded cleats, the whole of clear stuff.

23

WAINSCOT. Wainscot the walls of the kitchen and wash-room 3 feet in height with clear, narrow, beaded, vertical sheathing, neatly capped.

WOODEN MANTEL. Put up a neat wooden mantel, of marble pattern, in the large attic bed-room.

OUTSIDE BLINDS. Provide all the windows, except those of cellar and attic, with plain, neat Venetian blinds, in two and three panels each as their size requires, furnished with narrow rolling slats. Hang on the best blind hinges, and fasten with the most approved patent fastening.

FENCE. Build a fence across the rear and on one side of the lot, from the rear to the front house line, extending in all a distance of 145 feet, with squared chestnut posts set 3 feet 6 inches in the ground, and covered 7 feet high with sound merchantable mill-worked fence boards, neatly capped.

WASH-TRAY. Fit up the wash-trays in wash-room with 2-inch plank and 1¼-inch hinged plank cover, planed up and put together with white lead joints.

## PAINTING.

Properly stop and otherwise prepare for and paint all the planed wood work outside and inside of the building, and upon the premises that it is customary and usual to paint, (including the piazza floor and outside steps, the iron cresting, and the cutting in of the stairs), three good coats of the best American white lead and oil paint.

Paint the kitchen fire-place, the chimney shafts where exposed to exterior view, and the outside of the brick underpinning two coats.

Paint the tin-work of the roofs two good coats of the best metallic roof paint. Finish the roofs of the dormers, imitating the color of the slate.

Paint the fence one good heavy coat of ochre, colored as directed.

Finish all other portions of the work in color as directed.

Grain the wood-work of the kitchen and wash-room in imitation of light oak, and varnish one good coat.

GAS PIPES.     Put in all the required gas pipes ready for the fitters.    The work to be done in accordance with the requirements and regulations of the Brooklyn Gas Light Company.

GENERAL
SUMMARY.

All the work to be executed in the best manner, and to the entire satis-faction of the Architect.    The materials to be the best quality of their several kinds, when not otherwise specified.

Execute any and all further carpenter work necessary to fully complete the building fit and ready for occupation, which may be shown by, or is to be reasonably inferred from, the drawings, though not herein specified.

Remove all carpenters' waste material and rubbish from the premises at the completion; scrub the floors and wash the windows.

25

# DESIGN No. 10.

# MASONS' SPECIFICATION.

————————————— ▶•●•◀ —————————————

EXCAVATION.
Remove the top soil at the commencement, and replace it over the graded surface at the completion.

Excavate for a cellar under the entire building as shown on cellar plan, the depth figured on the section ; also, excavate 3 feet 6 inches deep for the piers supporting piazza posts, and the sills of front steps. Grade off the earth around the building, or remove it from the premises, as may be directed by the owner.

STONE WALLS.
Build the cellar walls of good flat building stone 20 inches thick, laid in hydraulic ground lime and clean sharp sand mortar. Build foundations for the chimneys, piazza and step piers in a similar manner. Put down concrete footings 8 inches deep, and extending in width at least 6 inches beyond the thickness of the walls on each side, under all the walls of the building ; the concrete composed of small broken stone, gravel, sand and cement, in the usual proportions.

Build both sides of the stone walls by and full to a line, finish in height level with the grade, and properly flush and point the inner face at the completion.

Put flat stone foundations under the cellar piers supporting girder.

BRICK WORK.
From the top of the stone walls at the grade level build a brick wall 12 inches thick and 7 courses in height. The wall to be flush on the inner face with the stone wall below.

Build the chimneys and cellar ash pit as per plans. Carry up the flues or uniform size and smoothly pargetted throughout. A ventilating flue with register opening near the ceiling line in kitchen to be carried up in the rear stack, between the two smoke flues.

The two flank chimneys to be topped out above the roof as per elevation and detail drawings, the remaining one on the ridge to top out plain.

Build the girder piers in cellar 12 inches square and cap with blue stone. Build the piers supporting piazza posts 8 inches square.

All the above-mentioned brick work to be executed with the best hard-burnt common brick laid up wet, with hydraulic ground lime and clean sharp sand mortar. Face the topping out of the chimneys, the throat, breast and jambs of the kitchen fire-place, and the exterior of the cellar walls, with selected, perfectly formed brick, the joints flushed full and rubbed preparatory to painting.

Turn trimmer arches against all the hearths, and furnish all the required rough brick, mortar and plaster for setting the hearths, grates, mantels and range.

COAL SLIDE.    Build the coal slide shown; line with smooth flag, provide with flag cover with round iron movable grating fastened with chain, staple and padlock.

NOGGING.    Fill in the entire frame below the attic floor with pale brick on edge laid in mortar with the joints flushed full.

CONCRETE FLOOR.    Cover the cellar floor flush and smooth throughout, 3 inches deep with concrete in the usual manner.

BLUE STONE.    Provide the cellar windows with blue stone sills 4 inches rise, 5 inches bed and the required length. Furnish the kitchen fire-place with rubbed blue stone hearth of the size shown on the plans, and not less than $3\frac{1}{2}$ inches thick. Provide smooth dressed flags, 2 feet in width by the required length, and bed in sand at the foot of the front and rear outside steps.

Lath the cellar ceiling and plaster one good coat.

Lath the walls and ceilings of the 1st and 2d stories throughout, and the attic hall and front bed room, and plaster three coats; scratch, brown and hard-finish with the best materials.

Finish off a neat plain dome over main stairway, with small mouldings at the angles; the size indicated on the plans.

Run moulded cornices of about 7 inches rise and 10 inches projection in the parlor and dining-room, and 5 inches rise and 8 inches projection in the halls and in 2d story principal rooms.

Put up neat centre-pieces of such pattern as the owner may select, of appropriate size, in the parlor, main hall and dining-room.

The plastering in the kitchen and wash-room to extend down to the grounds of the wainscot capping; in all other cases, to extend down to the floors and up to the grounds of the openings.

The walls in all cases to be finished plumb and the ceilings level, the angles to be maintained sharp and regular in line.

Do all necessary patching and mending made necessary by the plumbers, gas-fitters, bell-hangers and other workmen.

**STONE LINTEL.** Provide the kitchen fire-place with rubbed stone lintel of 8 inches rise and 4 inches bed by the required length.

**CESS-POOL.** Stone up where directed a cess-pool of 3 feet diameter and 12 feet deep, to receive the drainage from the house and the discharge from the roof leaders. Make the necessary connections to the building for that purpose through 6 inch vitrified or cement drain pipe, laid below the action of the frost and properly trapped.

**CLEANSING, &c.** Remove all rubbish and waste material from the premises that may have been accumulated by the Mason during the progress of the work, and leave building and premises broom clean at the completion.

**GENERAL SUMMARY.** Any Masons' work not herein specified, and necessary to complete the work in accordance with a fair and reasonable interpretation of the drawings as to their true meaning and intent, is to be executed by the contractor without extra charge, not, of course, including any alterations from or additions to the present design.

The entire work to be executed in the best and and most workmanlike manner, to the entire satisfaction of the Architect.

## MEMORANDA OF PAYMENTS ON CONTRACT.

(1). 10 PR. CT. When the entire frame of the building is raised, ready for the roof plank.

(2). 15 " " " building is enclosed, the roof on, and chimneys topped out.

(3). 20 " " " floors are laid, partitions set, brown coat on, and piazza and fences up.

(4). 20 " " " plastering is completed, with cornices, &c., run, exterior work finished and painted, and rough plumbing in.

(5). 35 " " " whole is completed and this contract fulfilled.

29

# DESIGN No. 10

# PLUMBERS' SPECIFICATION.

—————————▸◂◆▸◂—————————

IRON SOIL PIPE.    From the earthen drain-pipe connected with cesspool, extend within the cellar, and from thence up to the water-closet in second story, with a 4-inch cast-iron soil pipe, connected with the closet with 3-inch lead soil pipe and trap. Put up this pipe with iron holdfasts, and caulk all the joints water-tight with lead.

SUPPLY PIPE.    Tap, and pay for tapping the Ridgewood main, and connect, through 1-inch extra strong lead pipe, with boiler in kitchen.

BOILER.    Furnish, and set on iron stand in the kitchen, a 50-gallon copper boiler of the best construction, well hooked and soldered, and smoothly planished. Connect with the brass pipes of the water-back of the range, through one-inch copper pipes.

KITCHEN SINK.    Furnish and put up a 30 × 20 × 6 inch cast-iron sink in kitchen, where indicated on the plans, and supply it with hot and cold water through ⅝-inch strong supply pipes, ⅝-inch finished flange bibb cocks, 3-inch waste pipe, and 3-inch trap and brass trap screw. Furnish a lead branch and stopcock below the sink, for emptying the boiler.

WASH-TRAYS.    Supply three wash-trays in wash room, as per plans, with hot and cold water through ⅝-inch strong lead pipe and ⅝-inch finished flange and thimble-tray draw cocks. Put in strainers, plugs and chains, and connect the over flow of one tray with waste pipe. Supply with 3-inch main lead waste

30

pipe trapped and connected with the iron soil pipe, and connected with two-inch branch wastes from each tray.

FURNACE SUPPLY. Supply the furnace with cold water through ½-inch strong lead pipe, a 24 × 12 × 12 inch cistern, lined with four-pound lead, a four-pound copper ball and ball cock, and connect with the evaporator by a copper pipe.

WATER-CLOSET. Furnish, and set in the second story, where shown in the plans, a best-constructed pan closet, with white marble-pattern basin of Wedgewood-ware, enameled receiver, and silver-plated cup and handle. Provide with 24 × 14 × 14 inch cistern, lined with four-pound sheet lead, and furnished with box, valve, wire, five-pound copper ball, ball cock, etc., complete. Make the closet trap of 6-pound sheet lead.

SLOP SINK. By the side of water closet, furnish and fit up a best-ware slop-basin, properly supplied with water and cock, and wasted through 3-inch trapped waste pipe.

BATH. Furnish and put up in second story, as per plans, an eighteen-ounce sheet copper bath tub, tinned and planished, and supply with hot and cold water through ⅝-inch strong lead pipe, ⅝-inch silver plated flange cocks, and put in 1½-inch waste, properly trapped. Provide with silver-plated plug and chain.

STOP COCKS, ETC. Put in all necessary stop cocks that may be requisite or directed. Properly trap and grade all the pipes. Furnish all pipe necessary to supply, empty and connect the several works.

RANGE. Furnish, and set in kitchen fireplace, a No. 2 Knickerbocker range, with water-back, etc., complete.

WORKMANSHIP. The whole of the work to be done in the best manner known to the trade.

31

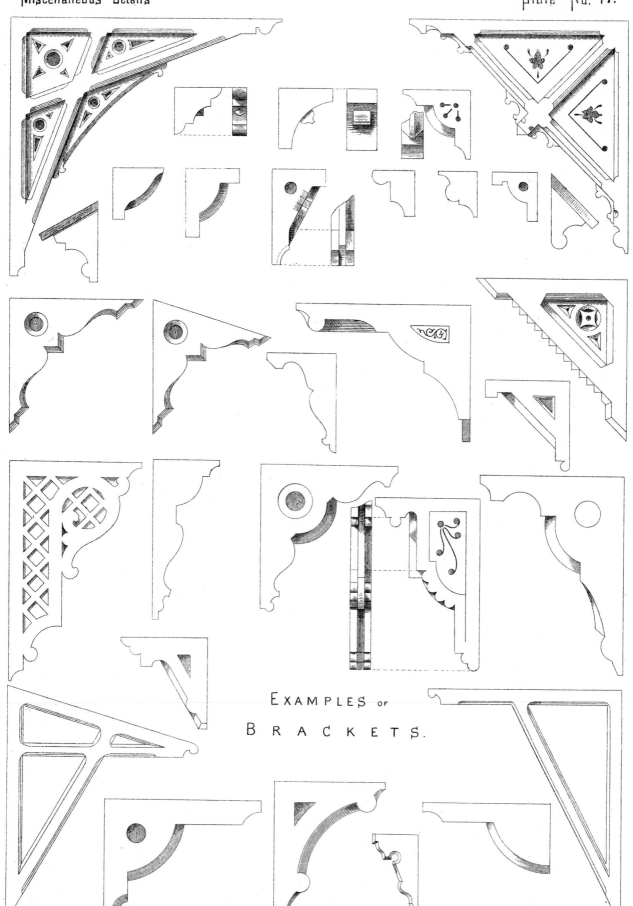

EXAMPLES of

B R A C K E T S.

EXAMPLES OF LATTICE WORK.

SCALE. ½ Inch to One Foot.

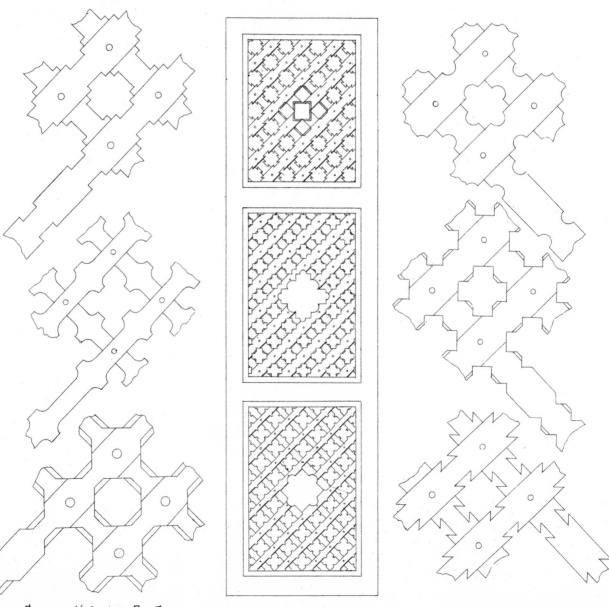

SCALE. ½ Inch to One Foot.

SCALE. ½ Inch to One Foot.

Design No. 11.                    Plate No. 50.

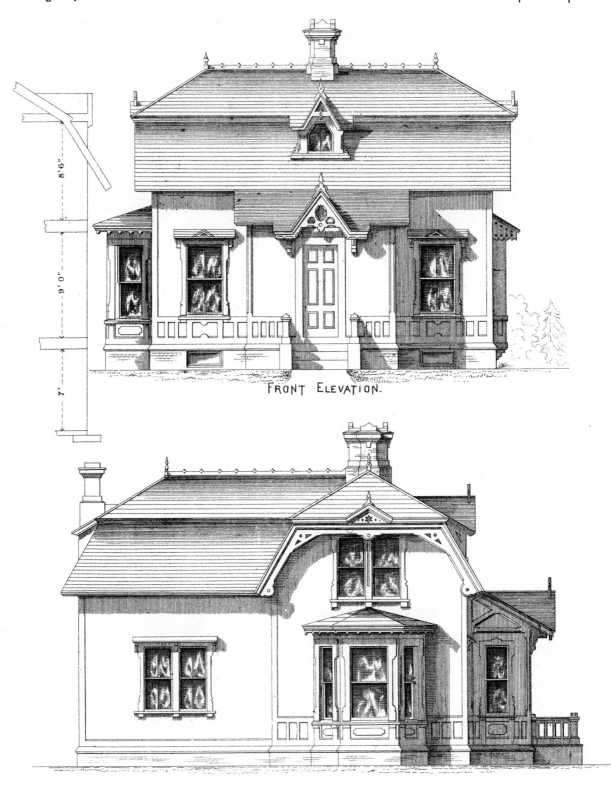

8'6"
9'0"
7'

FRONT ELEVATION.

SIDE ELEVATION.

SCALE. ⅛ Inch to One Foot.

Design No. 11.  Plate No. 51.

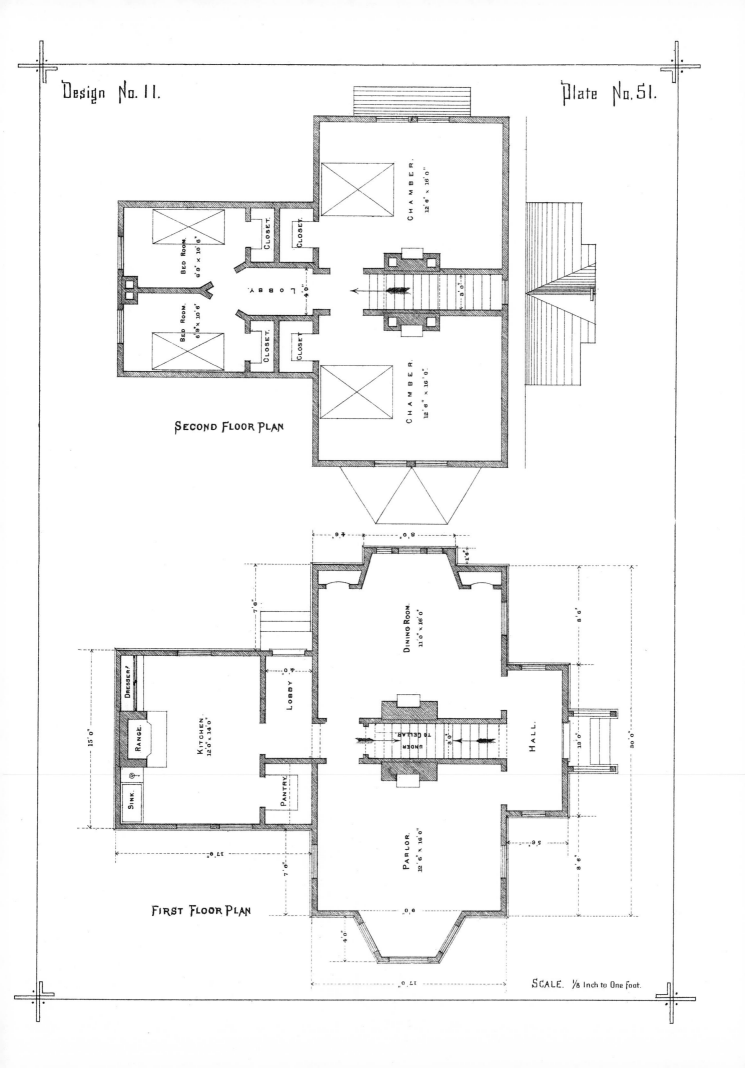

CHAMBER.
12'6" x 16'0"

BED ROOM.
6'9" x 10'6"

CLOSET.
CLOSET.

LOBBY.
4'0"

8'0"

BED ROOM.
6'9" x 10'6"

CLOSET.
CLOSET.

CHAMBER.
12'6" x 16'0"

SECOND FLOOR PLAN

DINING ROOM.
11'0" x 16'0"

9'6"  8'0"  1'6"

7'6"

8'6"

DRESSER.

LOBBY

4'0"

RANGE.

UNDER  3'0"  TO CELLAR.

HALL.

KITCHEN.
12'0" x 14'0"

15'0"

13'0"

30'0"

SINK.

PANTRY.

5'6"

17'0"

7'6"

8'6"

PARLOR.
12'6" x 16'0"

9'0"

FIRST FLOOR PLAN

4'0"

17'0"

SCALE. 1/8 Inch to One Foot.

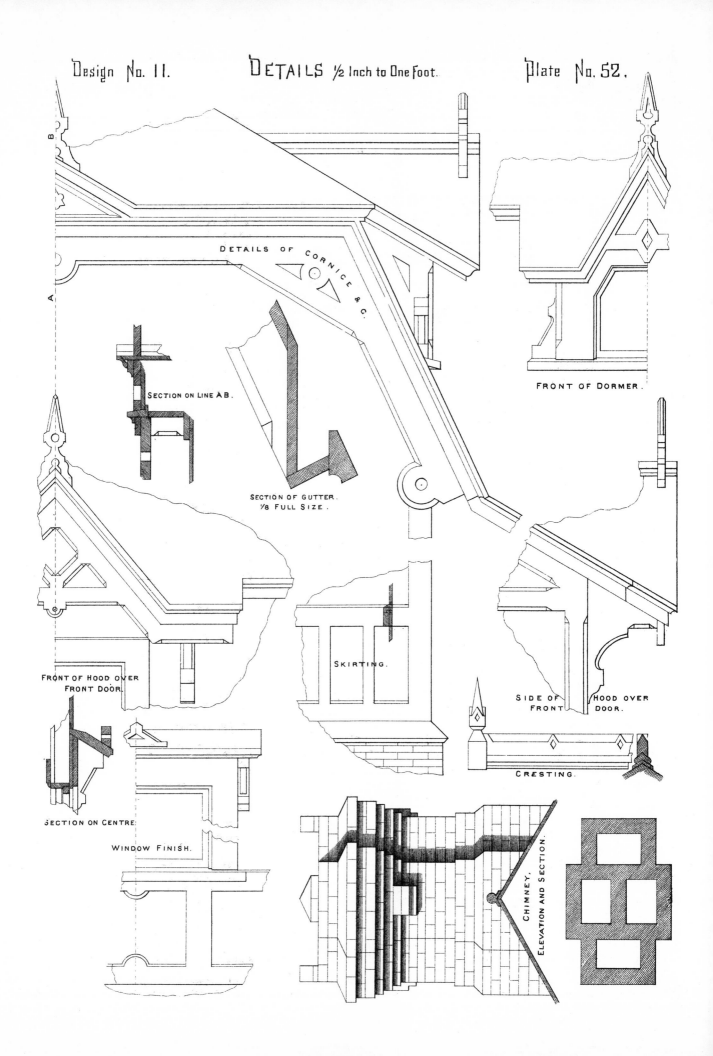

Design No. 11.   DETAILS ½ Inch to One Foot.   Plate No. 52.

DETAILS OF CORNICE &C.

SECTION ON LINE AB.

SECTION OF GUTTER.
⅛ FULL SIZE.

FRONT OF DORMER.

FRONT OF HOOD OVER
FRONT DOOR.

SKIRTING.

SIDE OF HOOD OVER
FRONT DOOR.

CRESTING.

SECTION ON CENTRE.

WINDOW FINISH.

CHIMNEY,
ELEVATION AND SECTION.

Design No. 12.                    Plate No. 53.

SIDE ELEVATION.

FRONT ELEVATION.

SCALE. ⅛ Inch to One Foot.

Design No. 12.                                                    Plate No. 54.

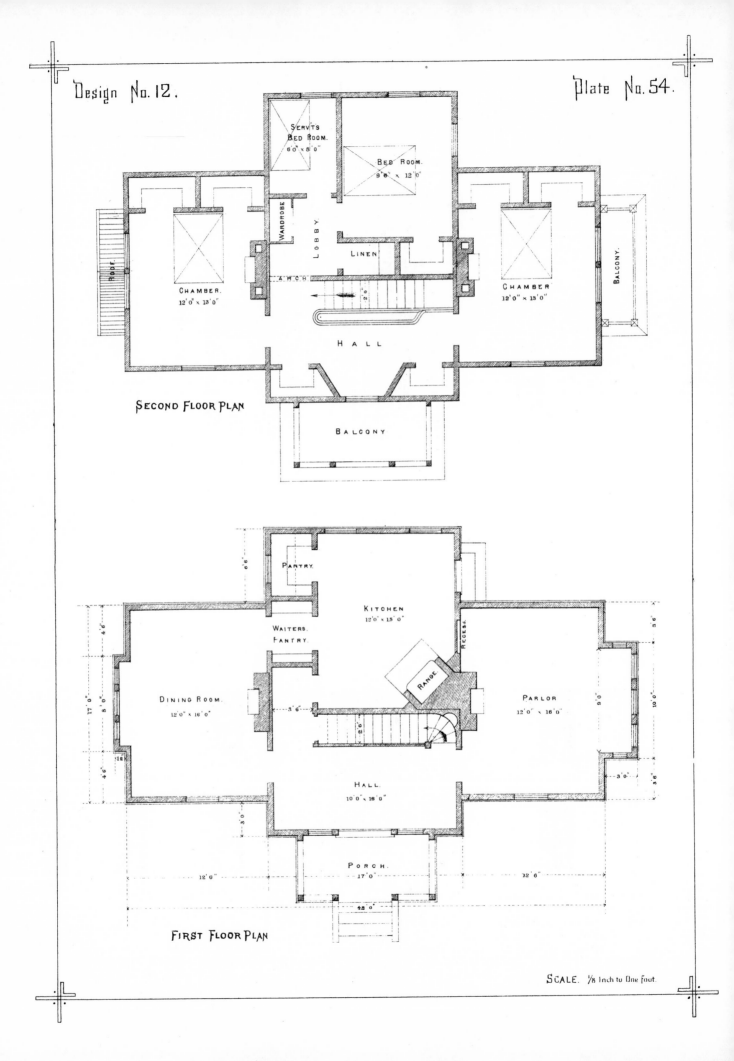

SERVTS
BED ROOM.
6'0" × 8'0"

BED ROOM.
9'6" × 12'0"

WARDROBE

LOBBY

LINEN

ARCH

ROOF

CHAMBER.
12'0" × 13'0"

CHAMBER.
12'0" × 13'0"

BALCONY.

2'0"

HALL

SECOND FLOOR PLAN

BALCONY

PANTRY.

6'6"

KITCHEN
12'0" × 15'0"

3'6"

4'6"

WAITERS.
PANTRY.

RECESS.

RANGE

PARLOR
12'0" × 18'0"

9'0"

10'0"

17'0"    8'0"

DINING ROOM.
12'0" × 16'0"

3'6"

3'6"

4'6"    12

3'6"

3'0"

HALL.
10'0" × 16'0"

3'0"

12'0"

PORCH.
17'0"

12'6"

45'0"

FIRST FLOOR PLAN

SCALE. 1/8 Inch to One Foot.

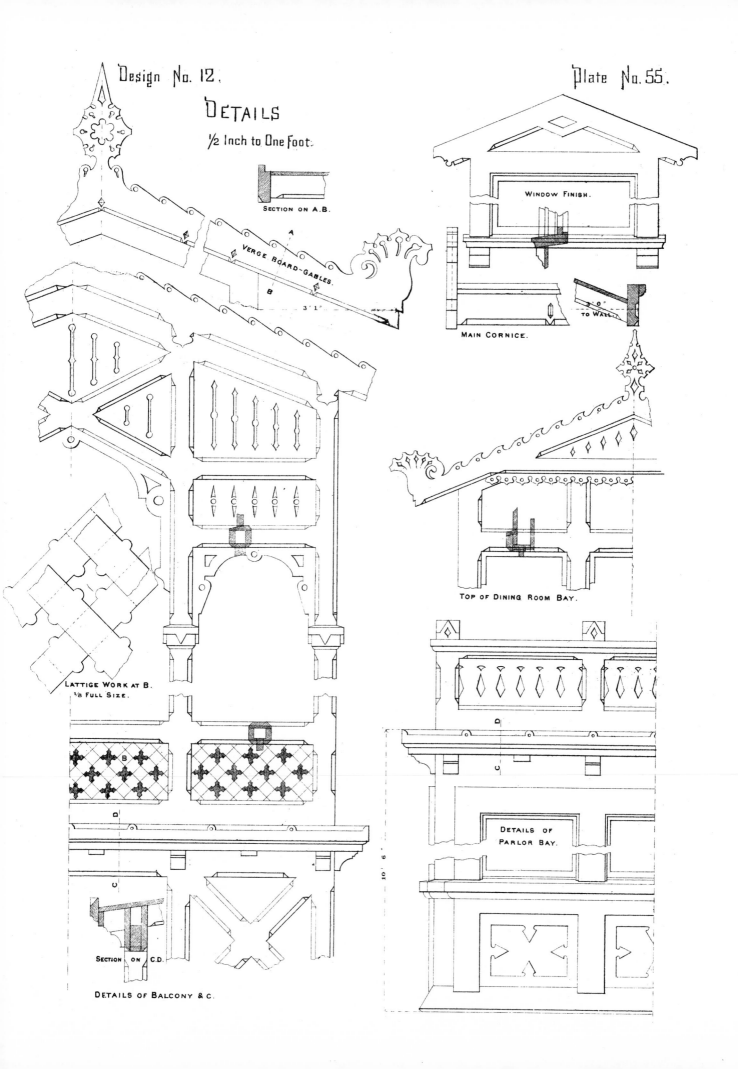

Design No. 12.

DETAILS

½ Inch to One Foot.

SECTION ON A.B.

VERGE BOARD-GABLES.

A
B
3' 1"

LATTICE WORK AT B.
⅛ FULL SIZE.

SECTION ON C.D.

DETAILS OF BALCONY &C.

Plate No. 55.

WINDOW FINISH.

MAIN CORNICE.

TO WALL

TOP OF DINING ROOM BAY.

DETAILS OF
PARLOR BAY.

Design No. 13.                                          Plate No. 56

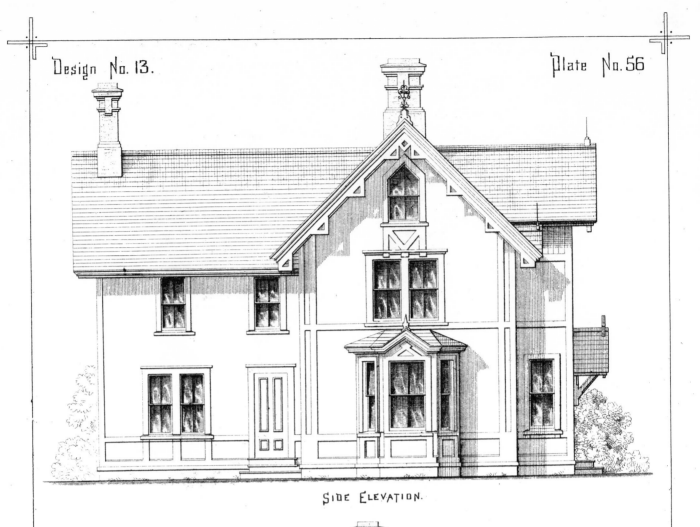

SIDE ELEVATION.

FRONT ELEVATION.

SCALE. 1/8 Inch to One Foot.

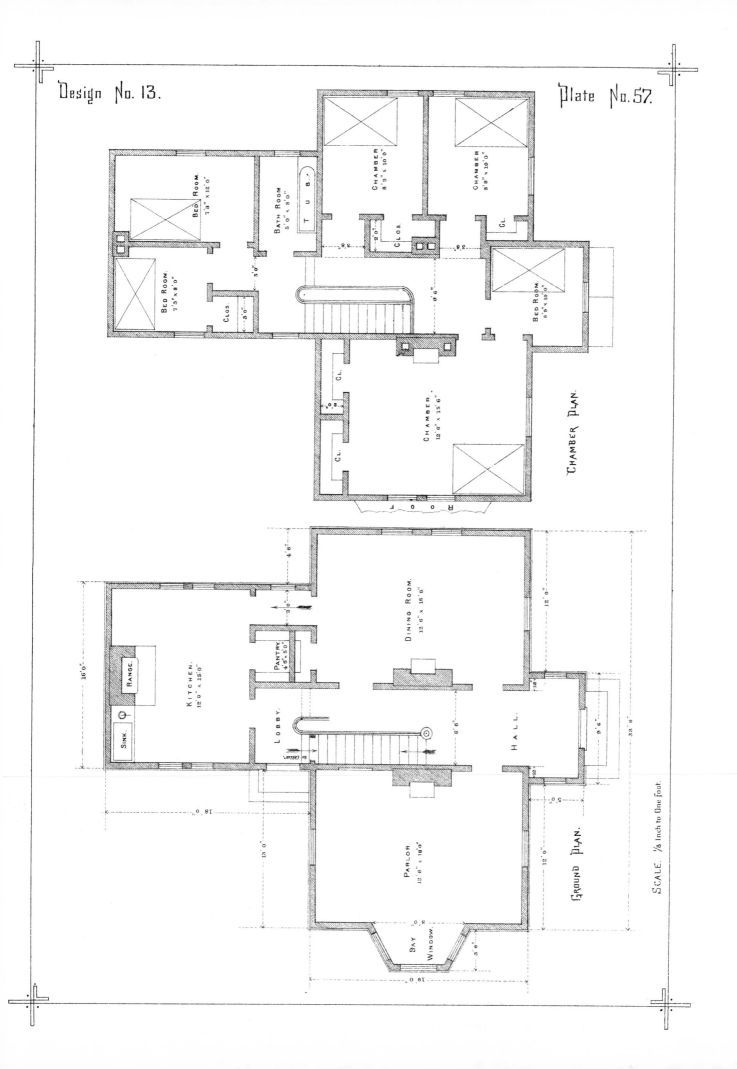

Design No. 13.

Plate No. 57.

BED ROOM
7'3" X 12'0"

BATH ROOM
5'0" X 8'0"

TUB

CHAMBER
8'9" X 10'0"

CHAMBER
8'9" X 10'0"

CLOS.

CL.

BED ROOM
7'3" X 8'0"

CLOS.

BED ROOM
8'6" X 10'0"

CL.

CHAMBER
12'6" X 15'6"

CL.

ROOF

CHAMBER PLAN.

RANGE.

SINK.

KITCHEN.
12'0" X 15'0"

PANTRY.
4'6" X 5'0"

LOBBY.

DINING ROOM.
12'6" X 18'0"

HALL.

PARLOR
12'6" X 18'0"

BAY WINDOW.

GROUND PLAN.

SCALE. ⅛ Inch to One foot.

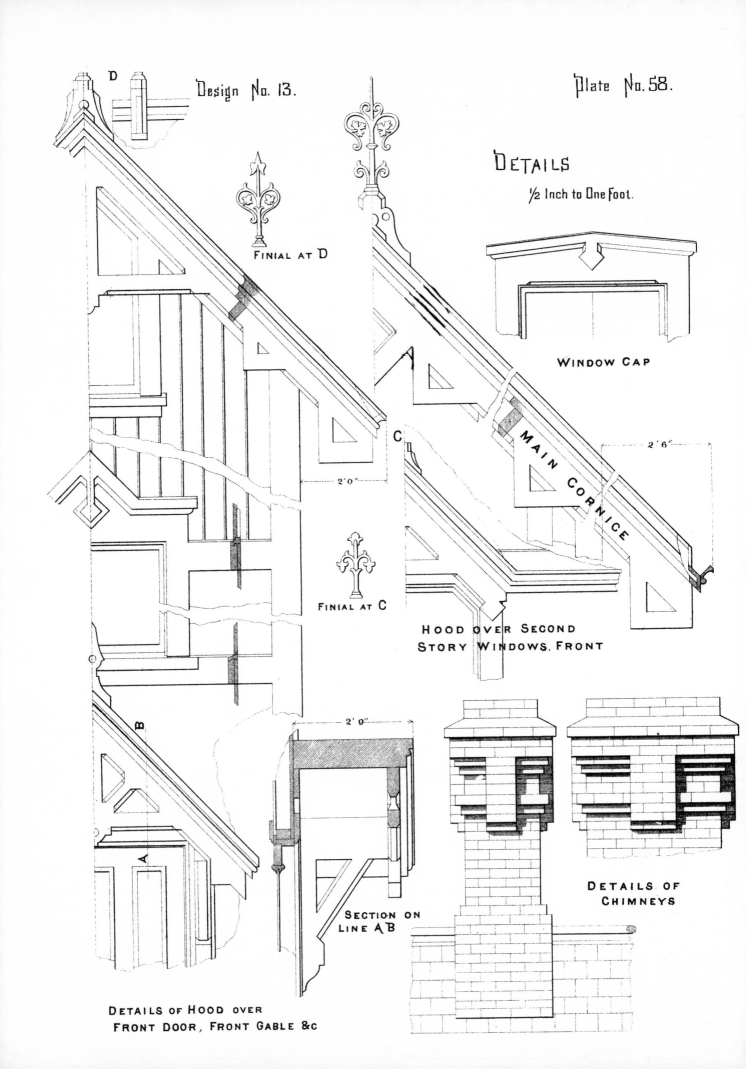

D

Design No. 13.

Plate No. 58.

FINIAL AT D

DETAILS

½ Inch to One Foot.

WINDOW CAP

C

2'0"

FINIAL AT C

MAIN CORNICE

2'6"

HOOD OVER SECOND
STORY WINDOWS, FRONT

B

2'0"

A

SECTION ON
LINE A B

DETAILS OF
CHIMNEYS

DETAILS OF HOOD OVER
FRONT DOOR, FRONT GABLE &c

Design No. 14.

Plate No. 59.

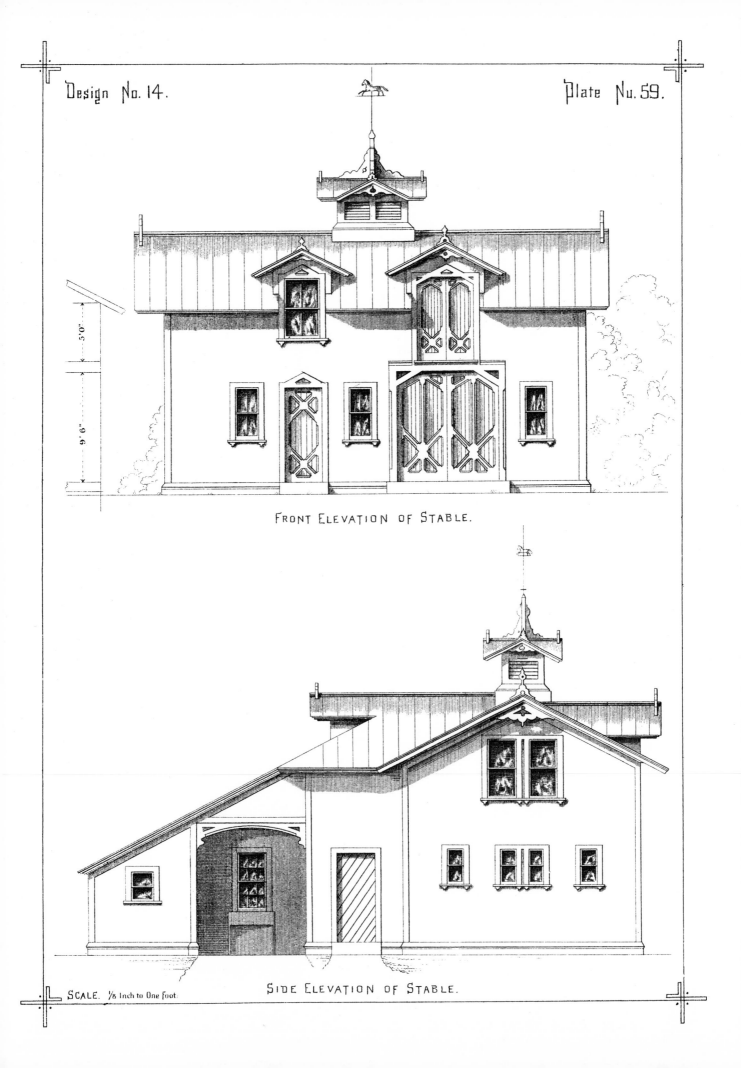

5'0"

9'6"

FRONT ELEVATION OF STABLE.

SIDE ELEVATION OF STABLE.

SCALE. 1/8 Inch to One Foot.

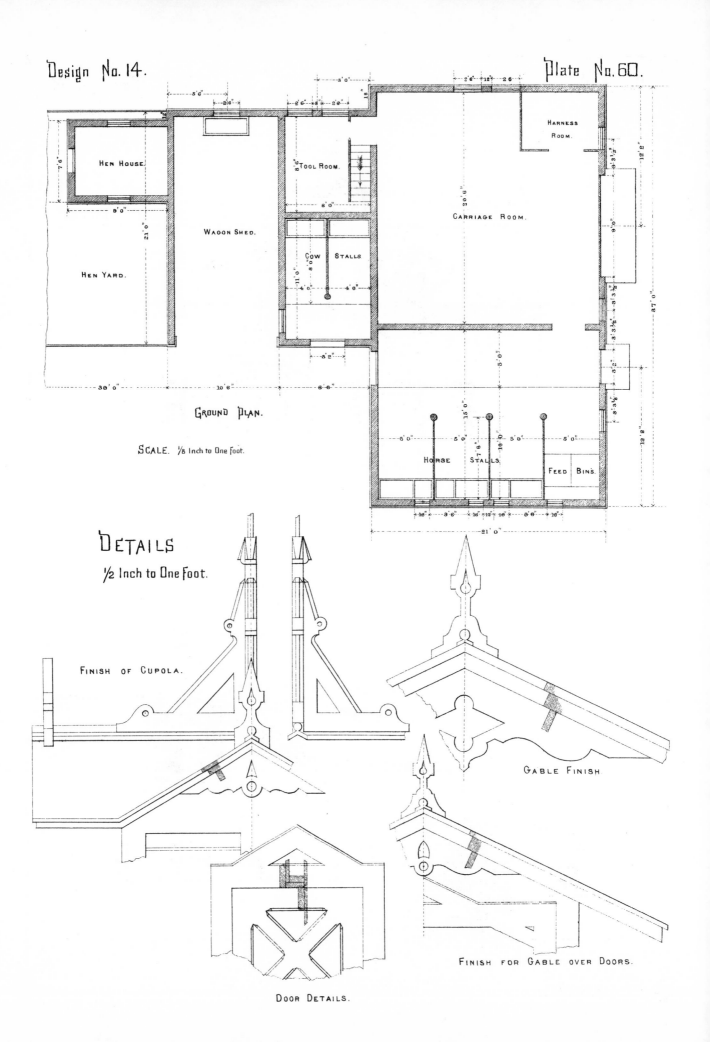

Design No. 14.                                                    Plate No. 60.

HEN HOUSE.

HEN YARD.

WAGON SHED.

TOOL ROOM.

COW STALLS

HARNESS ROOM.

CARRIAGE ROOM.

HORSE STALLS

FEED BINS.

GROUND PLAN.

SCALE. ⅛ Inch to One Foot.

DETAILS
½ Inch to One Foot.

FINISH OF CUPOLA.

GABLE FINISH

DOOR DETAILS.

FINISH FOR GABLE OVER DOORS.

Design No. 15.

FRONT ELEVATION.

7 INCHES TO THE FOOT

SCALE. 8 Feet to One Inch.

Design No. 15.

SIDE ELEVATION.

SCALE. 8 Feet to One Inch.

Design No. 15.                                    Plate No. 63.

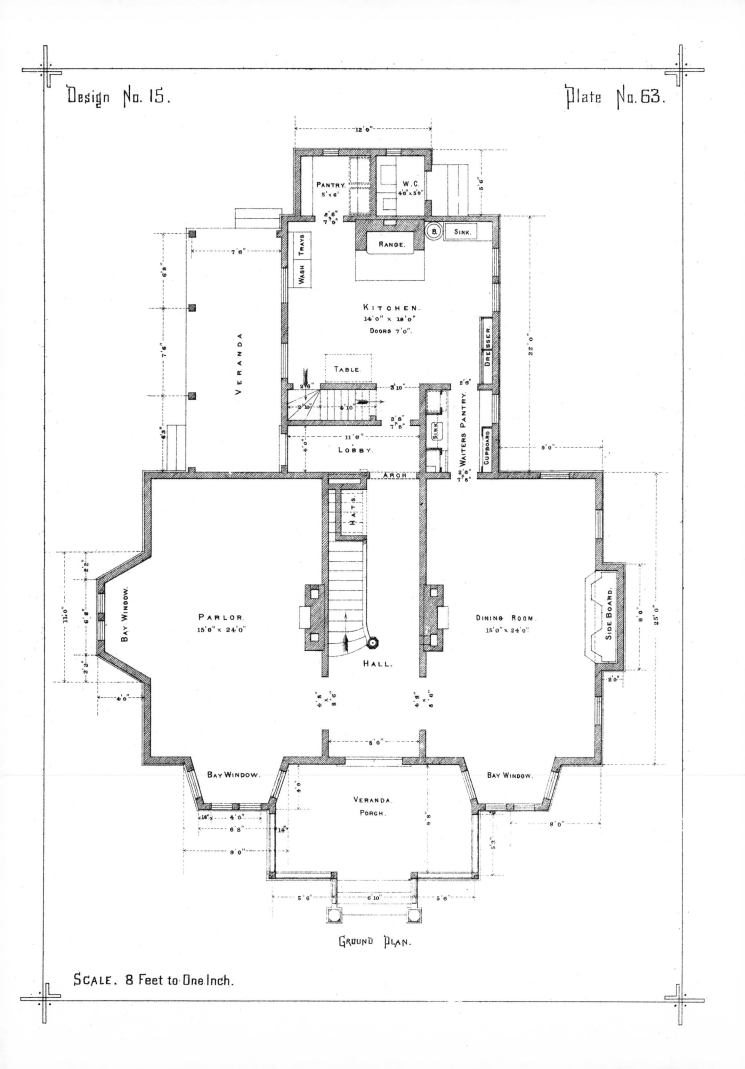

GROUND PLAN.

SCALE. 8 Feet to One Inch.

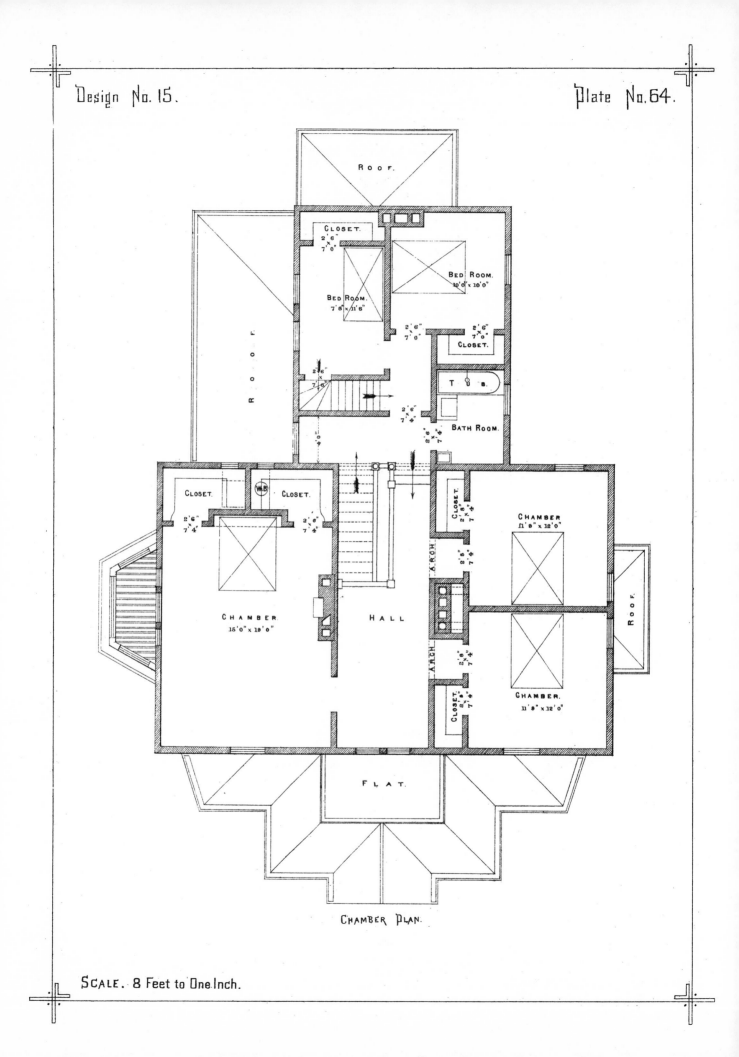

Design No. 15.

Plate No. 64.

ROOF.

CLOSET.
2'6"
x
7'0"

BED ROOM.
10'0" x 10'0"

BED ROOM.
7'6" x 11'6"

ROOF.

2'6"
7'0"

2'6"
x
7'0"

CLOSET.

2'6"
x
7'0"

TUB.

2'6"
7'0"

BATH ROOM.

2'6"
x
7'4"

CLOSET.

W.B.

CLOSET.

CLOSET.
2'8"
x
7'4"

CHAMBER
11'9" x 12'0"

2'6"
7'4"

2'6"
7'4"

HALL

CHAMBER.
15'0" x 19'0"

ARCH.

2'8"
7'4"

ROOF.

ARCH.

2'6"
7'4"

CLOSET.
2'8"
7'4"

CHAMBER.
11'9" x 12'0"

FLAT.

CHAMBER PLAN.

SCALE. 8 Feet to One Inch.

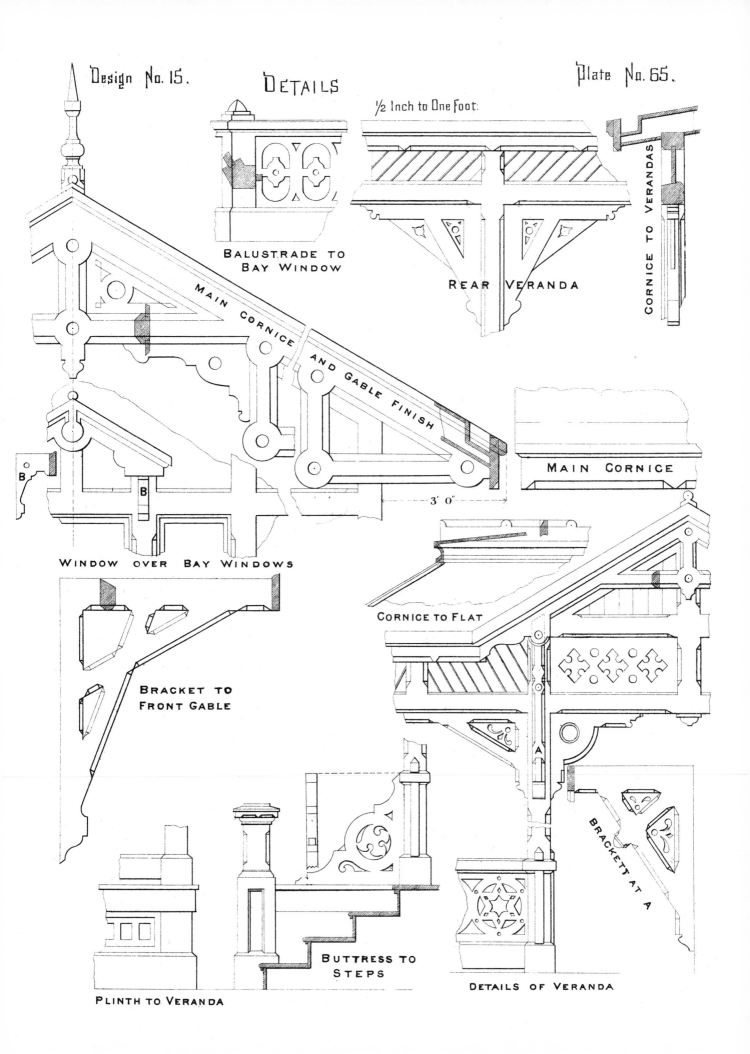

Design No. 15.    DETAILS    Plate No. 65.

½ Inch to One Foot:

BALUSTRADE TO BAY WINDOW

REAR VERANDA

CORNICE TO VERANDAS

MAIN CORNICE AND GABLE FINISH

3' 0"

MAIN CORNICE

WINDOW OVER BAY WINDOWS

CORNICE TO FLAT

BRACKET TO FRONT GABLE

BRACKETT AT A

BUTTRESS TO STEPS

PLINTH TO VERANDA

DETAILS OF VERANDA

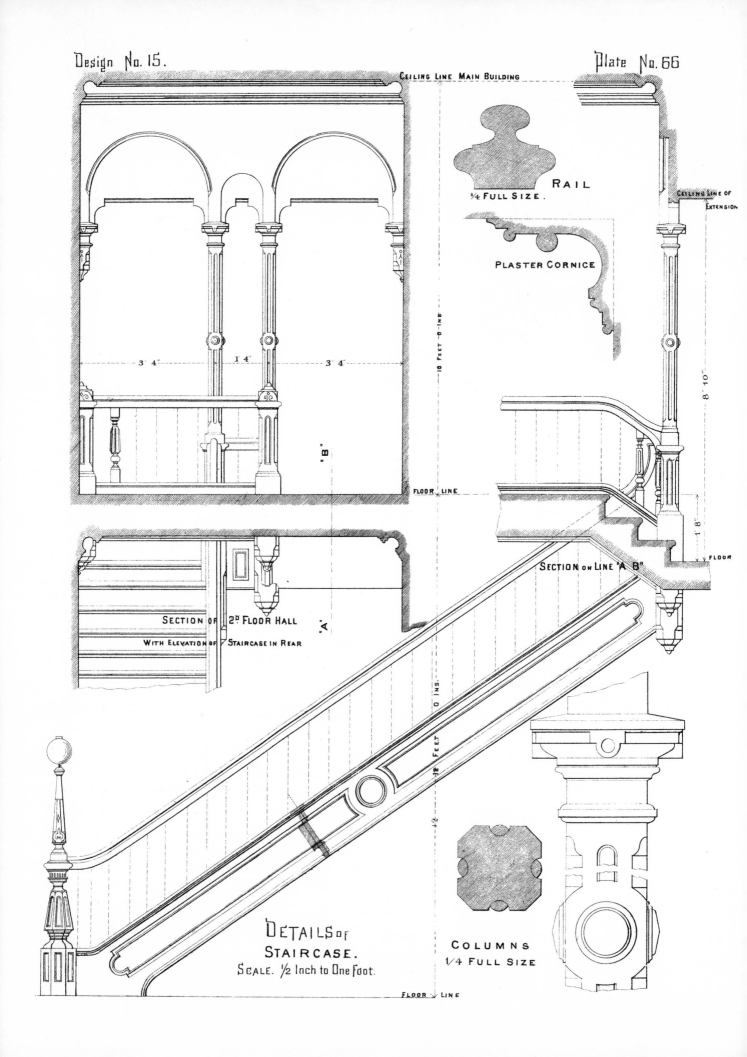

Design No. 15.

Plate No. 66

Ceiling Line Main Building

Ceiling Line of Extension

RAIL
¼ FULL SIZE.

PLASTER CORNICE

3' 4"    1' 4"    3' 4"

10 FEET 0 INS.

"B"

FLOOR LINE

8' 10"

1' 8"

FLOOR

SECTION ON LINE "A B"

SECTION OF 2ᴰ FLOOR HALL

WITH ELEVATION OF STAIRCASE IN REAR

"A"

12 FEET 0 INS.

DETAILS OF
STAIRCASE.
SCALE. ½ INCH TO ONE FOOT.

COLUMNS
¼ FULL SIZE

FLOOR LINE

Design No. 16

Plate No. 67.

FRONT ELEVATION.
SCALE. 0 ⅛ INCH TO ONE FOOT.

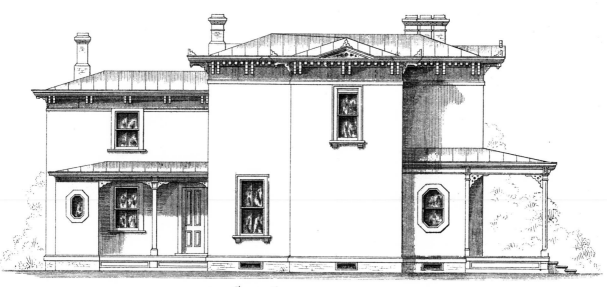

SIDE ELEVATION.
SCALE. 0 ³/₃₂ INCH. TO ONE FOOT.

1ST STORY ( MAIN BUILDING) 10'0" HIGH.
2D  „  „  9'0"  „
1ST  „  ( EXTENSION)  8'6"  „
2D  „  „  8'0"  „

Design No. 16                                      Plate No. 68.

13' 0"

W. C.

From Cellar

KITCHEN
12' x 12'

PIAZZA

19' 0"

10' 0"

18"

BOOKS

LIBRARY
9' x 9'

H.A.

DINING ROOM.
13' 8" x 14' 0"

9' 6"

BOOKS

13' 0"

CLOSET UNDER

HALL
9' 6" x 12'

H.A.

H.A.    H.A.

ARCH.

2' 0"

VESTIBULE
7' x 7' 6"

PARLOR.
14' x 16'

7' 6"

2' 0"

10' 0"

8' 0"

15' 0"

VERANDA

25' 0"

GROUND PLAN.

ROOF.

ROOF PLAN.

CLOSET.

SERVT'S BED ROOM.
12' x 12'

CLOSET.

BED ROOM.
9' x 9'

CHAMBER.
14' x 18'

CLOSET.

HALL.

CLOSET.

CLOSET.

WARDROBE.

PASSAGE.

WARDROBE.

CHAMBER.
14' x 13'

32' 0"

ROOF.

CHAMBER PLAN.

SCALE. 1/8 Inch to One Foot.

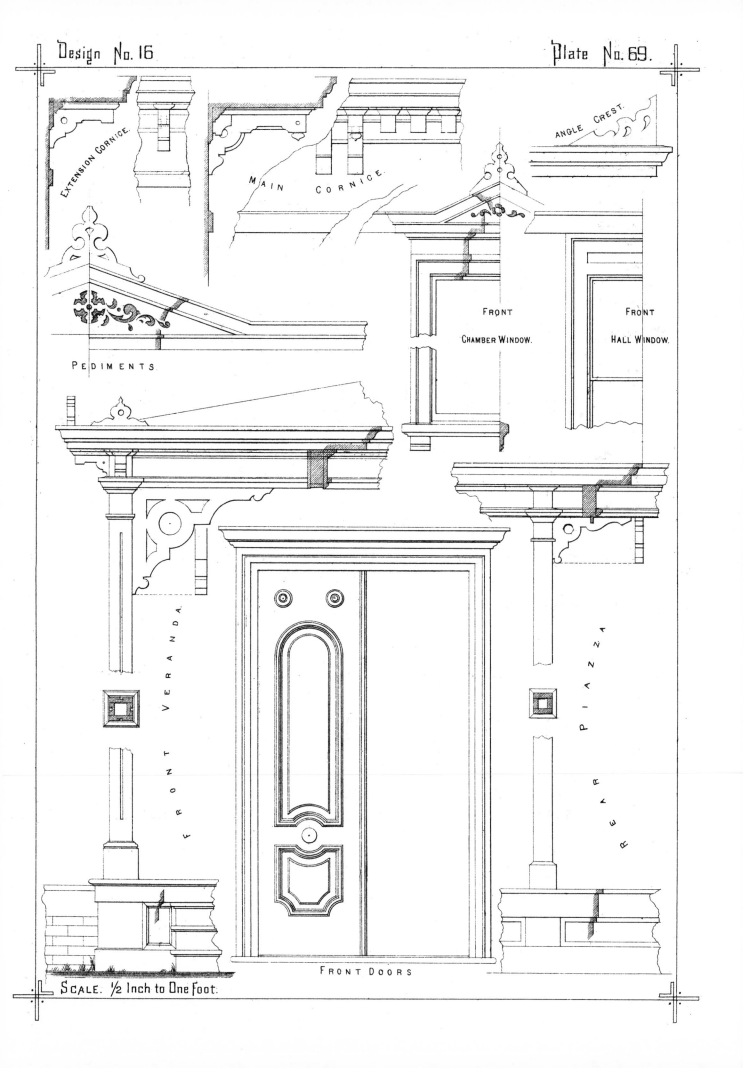

EXTENSION CORNICE.

MAIN    CORNICE.

ANGLE CREST.

PEDIMENTS.

FRONT
CHAMBER WINDOW.

FRONT
HALL WINDOW.

FRONT VERANDA.

REAR PIAZZA.

FRONT DOORS.

SCALE. 1/2 Inch to One Foot.

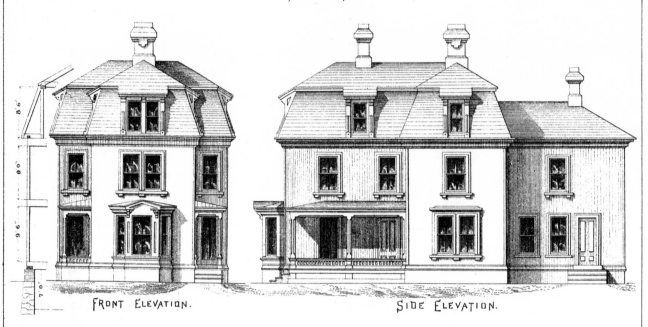

1/16 Inch to One Foot.

FRONT ELEVATION.                    SIDE ELEVATION.

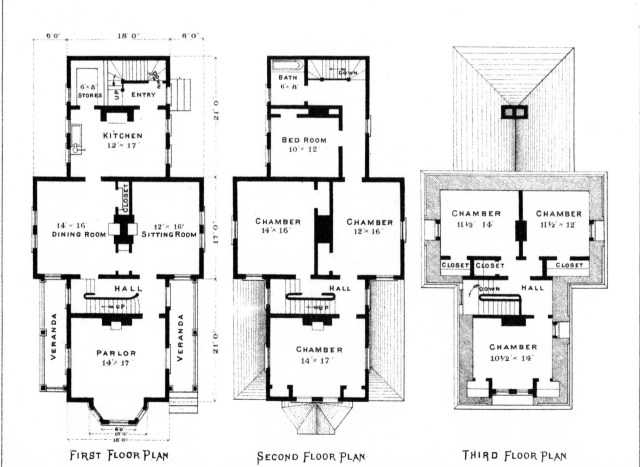

FIRST FLOOR PLAN          SECOND FLOOR PLAN          THIRD FLOOR PLAN

# DESIGN No. 17.

# MASONS' SPECIFICATION.

EXCAVATION.

Excavate for the cellar walls to the depth of 5 feet below the finished grade, for all the drains, to the depth of 3 feet, and do all the excavating required for the cistern and cess pool.

After the walls have been built, and the drains and other works specified have been set, fill up and grade off with the earth excavated, as may be directed.

STONE WORK.

Lay the cellar walls 20 inches thick, $5\frac{1}{2}$ feet high, with good large-sized building stone, laid in the best lime mortar. Start from a good firm foundation 6 inches below the finished level of the cellar bottom.

Point full with best mortar at the completion.

Level the cellar bottom and grout and cement it in the best manner.

CESS POOL

Build a cess pool 3 feet in diameter and 6 feet deep, as directed, with good building stone laid dry. Cover with sound chestnut plank 4 inches thick.

PIERS.

Set proper stone foundations for the brick piers herein specified, those on the outside set 3 feet deep.

CUT STONE.

Provide and set blue stone sills, 4 × 6 inches, for all the cellar windows, also, dressed blue stone hearth and lintel for the kitchen fire-place.

DRAINS.
Lay one 4-inch drain from beneath the sink in the kitchen to the cess pool, and one of the same calibre from the cistern to the cess pool, to serve as an overflow pipe. Both of the above to be properly trapped.

Lay 4-inch drain pipes from the leaders to the cistern.

All of the above to be of vitrified earthen pipe, with all angle pieces required, set with cemented joints, and connected with cistern, cess pool, &c., in the best manner.

## BRICK WORK.

UNDERPINNING.
Lay the underpinning walls 2 feet high and 12 inches thick.
Set window frames as required by the design.

PIERS.
Build three 12-inch square brick piers to carry the timbers in the first floor, and four 8-inch square piers to carry the veranda floors.

Use best cement for the external piers.

CHIMNEYS
Build the chimneys as required by the design. Faced work in the kitchen fire-place of selected bricks, with flushed joints, rubbed. Grate fire-places elsewhere as the plans show. Flues 8 × 12 inches, pargetted throughout. Top out the chimneys above the roof as required by the design, using selected bricks, with best cement, and flush and rub the joints.

Furnish and set three marble mantels, with Dixon's low down grates, of the value of —— dollars each, and one range, of medium size and of approved manufacture.

Turn trimmer arches for all the hearths.

CISTERN.
Build a cistern at the rear of the house as directed, 8 feet in diameter and 6 feet deep in the clear, the bottom of the cistern being $8\frac{1}{2}$ feet below the finished surface. Build the vertical walls, and the top (domical in form) 4 inches thick. Man-hole 2 feet in diameter, inside, and carried up to the surface.

Grout and cement the bottom in the best manner. Lay all the brick work with cement, and finish all the interior, as well as the outside of the domed top and the man-hole, with two coats of best cement.

Cover the man-hole with 3-inch stone slab and rim, the former fitted with iron ring and staple.

BRICK FILLING.    Fill in the frame work of the exterior walls their entire height with good pale bricks, set on edge, flush with the inner edge of the studding.

## MATERIALS FOR BRICK WORK.

Except for the filling in, use for all the brick work specified herein good hard-burned weather bricks.

Select the best of them for exposed face work, and, except as otherwise specified herein, lay all bricks with best lime and sand mortar.

## LATHING AND PLASTERING.

Lath the ceilings, the walls of the 3d story, and the partitions throughout, with good, sound laths, and plaster with one good, heavy coat of hair mortar, finished with " hard finish " white coat.

Float, smooth and finish the plastering throughout in the best manner.

DEAFENING.    Deafen the first floor by grouting between the beams.

Limewash the whole interior of the cellar, including the bottom of the first floor, two good coats.

# DESIGN No. 17.

# CARPENTERS' SPECIFICATION.

---

### FRAME.

Furnish all timber required to execute the framing, according to the design. Flooring beams to be of spruce; remainder of the timber of pine or hemlock, and all sound and square edged.

Sizes of the parts as follows :

Sills, 3 × 8 inches, halved at the angles and well nailed.

Flooring beams, 2 × 9 inches.

Trimmers and headers, 4 × 9 inches.

Girders carrying ends of beams, in first floor, 6 × 9 inches.

Corner studs, 4 × 4 inches.

Window and door studs, 3 × 4 inches, and remaining wall studs, 2 × 4 inches.

Plates, 3 × 4 inches.

Rafters for Mansard roof, 2 × 6 inches; for upper roof, 2 × 8 inches.

Ceiling pieces for third story, 2 × 6 inches.

Sills for veranda floors, 4 × 6 inches.

Joists, 2 × 6 inches.

Veranda plates, 3 × 6 inches.

Rafters, 3 × 5 inches.

Execute the framing in the manner commonly known as "Balloon Framing," and in the most substantial and skillful manner.

Bridge all the flooring beams with one row of 1 × 3 crossed bridging Double the beams that carry partitions.

## EXTERIOR COVERING.

WALLS.

Cover all the vertical walls with pine sheathing, planed $\frac{7}{8}$-inch thick, matched, and set in widths of not more than 5 inches.

ROOFS.

Cover the roofs with sound matched roofing boards. Select the best of them for the verandah roofs and plain the under side of them for the latter, and bead and scratch bead.

TIN WORK.

Line the gutters throughout, extending the lining up at least 6 inches under the slates.

Finish the veranda and bay window roofs with tin, put on with standing lock joints, and turned up at least 2 inches behind the siding. Carry the tin work of the bay window roof up and back of the siding 6 inches, and make weather-tight.

Put up 4 leaders of $3\frac{1}{2}$ inches calibre on the walls of the house. Also, 1 leader of $2\frac{1}{2}$ inches calibre on each of the verandas, and 1 of the same size on the bay window. All of these leaders to connect at the top with the gutters, and at the bottom with the drains, and to be properly secured to the walls with metallic fastenings.

Use the best quality of charcoal roofing tin for all of the above specified tin work, and paint it all with two good coats of best metallic roofing paint.

SLATING.

Finish all the roofs, not required above to be tinned, with good sound black or purple slates, over stout roof felting, the slates laid so that each course shall lap the second course below it $2\frac{1}{2}$ inches.

39

Flash the hips, valleys, ridges and chimneys with stout zinc, and make all the roof weather proof.

**SCUTTLE.** Set glazed scuttle two by three feet in the roof as directed, and hang it with wrought iron hinges and hasp.

**EXTERIOR FINISH.** Put up the cornices, window and door finish, corner beads, and water table, as required by the design. (See "cornice, corner bead and water table" in Plate 82.) Case up gutters in the cornices. Plane and bead the timber in the roof of the verandas. Make the veranda railings of $1\frac{1}{4}$-inch pine, cut as shown, and with proper cap and plinth. Veranda floors of $1\frac{1}{4}$-inch pine, planed, matched, set in widths of four inches, with leaded joints, and blind nailed.

Outside steps of similar workmanship. Build the bay-window as required by the design. Brackets for pediment three inches thick.

Water-table $1\frac{1}{2}$ inches thick. Lip the top edge to connect with the siding. Band mouldings for windows and doors three inches wide, $1\frac{1}{4}$ inches thick, with coved inner edge. Cover the top band with metal or wooden cap so as to make it weather proof.

Window sills two and one-half inches thick.

Dormer windows as the design requires. Brackets and finish at the sides 6 inches on the face, the latter raised 3 inches from the plane of the roof where it follows the line of the roof, and finished with $2\frac{1}{2}$-inch bead. Four inches margin between the edge of the window frame and the side finish. Double window sill, the lower one extending to the edge of the gutter, and covered with tin, as required for the roofs.

**BLINDS.** Provide outside blinds for all the windows in the first and second stories, and hang them with approved hinges and fastenings. Blinds to be $1\frac{1}{4}$ inches thick, four panels to each window, with rolling shades.

Do any and all other finishing work required to carry out the design as shown by the drawings.

40

## WINDOWS.

**CELLAR.**      Cellar window frames, six in number, of plank, rabbeted.

Sashes 1½ inches thick, hung at the top with iron butts, and fastened open and shut with strong iron buttons.

**FRAMES.**      Above the cellar, adapted for hanging the sashes with cords and weights.

**SASHES.**      One and a half inches thick, finished, two sashes to the window.

**GLASS.**      For all the windows throughout, of the sizes given on the drawings, and of the best quality of French sheet glass.

**HANGING.**      Double hang all the sashes with 2-inch best axle pulleys, iron weights, and best hemp sash cord, and put on spring centre fastenings of approved pattern, with white porcelain knobs. (French windows, opening on veranda, specified under the head of "Doors.")

## INTERIOR.

**FLOORS.**      Lay the floors throughout with thoroughly seasoned, perfectly sound flooring, 1¼ inches thick, set in widths not more than 5 inches to any one piece, planed, matched, and blind nailed.

Smooth off the floors after laying where required to reduce them to a uniform surface.

Saddles for all the doors of hard wood.

Case up an opening in the ceiling of the third story, in one of the closets, set a suitable cleated door, provide step-ladder communicating with it, and lay, with sound boards, a floor equivalent to ten feet square around the opening.

**DEAFENING.**      Furnish materials and do all carpenter's work required in deafening the first floor.

41

STAIRS.

Build the cellar stairs with 2-inch plank string pieces, and 1½-inch treads, planed and grooved together.

Build the rear stairs, from the first to the second story, with 1¼-inch risers and 1-inch treads. Enclose them with a partition of 1¼-inch planed, matched and beaded sheathing, carried down so as to enclose the cellar stairway, and carried up three feet above the second floor, surmounted with a 2½-inch bead.

Build the principal stairs, from the first to the third story, with 1¼-inch treads, finished with scotia and torus nosing, and 1-inch risers.

Set a 6-inch fancy turned newel at the start, and carry up a continued 2½ by 4-inch moulded rail, on plain turned balusters 1½-inch in diameter.

The post, rail, and balusters to be of the best seasoned black walnut rubbed down smooth, filled with oil, and finished with shellac.

PARTITIONS.

Set the partitions throughout as required by the plans. Studs 2 by 4 inches, set 16 inches on centres.

Studs for door jambs and projecting angles set double.

FIRRING

Firr down the ceilings, excepting that of the cellar, with 1 by 2 firring strips, set 16 inches on centres.

GROUNDS.

Set grounds around the window and door openings, and at the top of the base and skirting, to terminate the plastering.

Finish all projecting angles with corner beads.

## DOORS.

Make the front outside door 2 inches thick, with raised mouldings, and of the size given on the drawings. Rear entrance door 1¾ inches thick. Inside door for the first story 2 feet 10 inches by 7 feet, and for the second and third stories 2 feet 8 inches by 6 feet 10 inches, four panels to the door 1½ inches thick, with beveled stiles and rails.

Glaze the two upper panels of the rear entrance door with best French sheet glass, and those of the front door with ornamental enamelled glass.

42

# CARPENTERS' SPECIFICATION.—DESIGN NUMBER SEVENTEEN

**FRENCH WINDOWS.**

Sashes for French windows, which include all the windows opening on the verandas, 1¾ inches thick. Stiles and top rail 2½ inches wide, meeting stile 4 inches wide, and bottom rail 6 inches wide.

Glaze with the best French sheet glass, three panes to each half window.

**HINGING.**

Hang the doors and the French windows with loose jointed iron butts of proper size.

Put in, in the French windows, approved locks, handles, and flush brass bolts.

Fasten the doors throughout with mortise locks and latches of best manufacture, with brass bolts and facings, and white porcelain furniture.

**BELL.**

Hang one bell in the kitchen, connected with the front door by copper wires in zinc tubes. Bell of the gong pattern.

**WINDOW AND DOOR FINISH.**

Trim the windows and doors throughout with plain casings from 5 to 6½ inches wide, with quarter round inner edge.

Finish the windows in the dining-room and sitting-room with framed and moulded panel backs, and the remaining windows with moulded stool pieces and aprons.

**BASE.**

Finish the rooms in the first story, not required to be wainscotted, with base 9½ inches high, all the rooms in the second story with base 9 inches high, those in the third story with base 8 inches high. Cove the upper edge of the base in the first story, and bevel it in the second and third stories one-half inch.

**WAINSCOT.**

Sheath up the walls of the kitchen, entry and pantry to the height of 3 feet from the floor, with pine sheathing, planed, matched, beaded, put up vertically in widths of 3 inches, and finished with neat moulded cap.

**PANTRY.**

Put up a shelf 20 inches wide across the end of the pantry, and fit up cupboards with shelves and cleated doors beneath it. Continue this shelf

43

along the sides of the pantry 14 inches wide, and put up three other shelves extending around the walls, and from 9 to 12 inches wide.

CHINA CLOSET.    Fit up the china closet with four shelves and three drawers, the latter 10 inches deep.

SHELVES.    Put up, on beaded cleats, one top shelf in each of the remaining closets, and double iron clothes hooks in closets and entries as directed.

MANTELS.    Build two wooden mantels, of the value of          dollars each, for the chambers over the dining-room and sitting-room.

SINK.    Furnish and set one cast-iron sink, 20 by 36 by 6 inches, in the kitchen. as by the plan.    Case up a cupboard under the same, with materials similar to those required for the wainscot, and set cleated door, properly hung and fastened.

PUMP.    Furnish and set a medium sized cast-iron pump next the sink, as required by the plan.    Connect with the cistern by means of a $1\frac{1}{2}$-inch lead supply pipe.    Put in a 2-inch lead waste pipe from the sink to the drain leading to the cess-pool.

BATH-TUB.    Furnish and set a copper planished, medium sized bath-tub, as by the plan.    Case up about it with pine sheathing, as for the kitchen wainscot, and carry a $1\frac{1}{2}$-inch lead waste pipe from the tub to the drain leading to the cesspool.

# PAINTING.

Paint all the exterior and interior wood-work, the chimney tops, and the faced brick-work about the kitchen fire-place, two good coats of best American white lead and pure linseed oil.    Paint the outside blinds three coats.    Tint as directed.

Properly putty all nail holes and other imperfections of the wood-work requiring it, and size all knots with gum shellac before painting.

## MATERIALS.

For the blinds, doors and sashes throughout, use the best clear white pine lumber.

For all the other wood finish, except where specified to the contrary herein, use white pine lumber, free from shakes, and large or bad knots.

All finishing materials to be perfectly sound and thoroughly seasoned.

The drawings herein referred to are to be considered as forming part of this specification, reference being made to them for the height of stories, and other dimensions, as well as for the general arrangement. And the contractor is to furnish all of the materials, and do all the labor required to complete the design, according to the evident intent of the drawings referred to and this specification; both the materials and the workmanship to be satisfactory to the Owner or his agent.

# APPROVED FORM OF CONTRACT IN GENERAL USE.

𝕬𝖗𝖙𝖎𝖈𝖑𝖊𝖘 𝖔𝖋 𝕬𝖌𝖗𝖊𝖊𝖒𝖊𝖓𝖙, made this           day
of           in the year one thousand eight hundred and

𝕭𝖊𝖙𝖜𝖊𝖊𝖓

**of the First Part,** and

**of the Second Part.**


FIRST. The said part    of the second part do    hereby for         heirs,
executors and administrators, covenant, promise and agree to and with the said part    of
the first part,         executors, administrators or assigns, that
the said part    of the second part         executors or administrators, shall
and will, for the consideration hereinafter mentioned, on or before the
well and sufficiently erect and finish the new Building

agreeably to the Drawings and Specifications made by
and signed by the said parties and hereunto annexed, within the time aforesaid, in a good,
workmanlike and substantial manner, to the satisfaction, and under the direction of the said
        to be testified by a writing or certificate under the hand of the
said         and also shall and will find and provide such good,
proper and sufficient materials, of all kinds whatsoever, as shall be proper and sufficient for
the completing and finishing all the

and other works of the said Building    mentioned in the         Specification
for the sum of

46

And the said part      of the first part, do      hereby, for                                    heirs, executors and administrators, covenant, promise and agree, to and with the said part      of the second part,                       executors and administrators, that the said part      of the first part                       executors or administrators, shall and will, in consideration of the covenants and agreements being strictly performed and kept by the said part      of the second part, as specified, well and truly pay, or cause to be paid, unto the said part      of the second part                       executors, administrators or assigns, the sum of

Dollars, lawful money of the United States of America, in manner following:

**Provided,** that in each of the said cases, a certificate shall be obtained and signed by the said

# And it is hereby further agreed by and between the said Parties:

FIRST.   The Specifications and Drawings are intended to co-operate, so that any works exhibited in the Drawings, and not mentioned in the Specifications, or *vice versa*, are to be executed the same as if they were mentioned in the Specifications and set forth in the Drawings, to the true meaning and intention of the said Drawings and Specifications, without any extra charge whatsoever.

SECOND.   The Contractor, at his own proper cost and charges, is to provide all manner of materials and labor, scaffolding, implements, moulds, models, and cartage of every description, for the due performance of the several erections.

THIRD.   Should the Owner, at any time during the progress of the said Building request any alteration, deviation, additions or omissions from the said contract, he shall be at liberty to do so, and the same shall in no way affect or make void the contract, but will be added to or deducted from the amount of the contract, as the case may be, by a fair and reasonable valuation.

FOURTH.   Should the Contractor, at any time during the progress of the said work, refuse or neglect to supply a sufficiency of materials and workmen, the Owner shall have the power to provide materials and workmen, after three days notice in writing being given, to finish the said work, and the expenses shall be deducted from the amount of the contract.

47

FIFTH. Should any dispute arise respecting the true construction or meaning of the Drawings or Specifications, the same shall be decided by                    and decision shall be final and conclusive; but should any dispute arise respecting the true value of the extra work, or of the works omitted, the same shall be valued by two competent persons—one employed by the Owner, and the other by the Contractor—and those two shall have power to name an umpire, whose decision shall be binding on all parties.

SIXTH. The Owner shall not, in any manner, be answerable or accountable for any loss or damage that shall or may happen to the said works, or any part or parts thereof respectively, or for any of the materials or other things used and employed in finishing and completing the same (loss or damage by fire excepted).

𝕴𝖓 𝖂𝖎𝖙𝖓𝖊𝖘𝖘 𝖜𝖍𝖊𝖗𝖊𝖔𝖋, the said parties to these presents have hereunto set their hands and seals, the day and year above written.

48

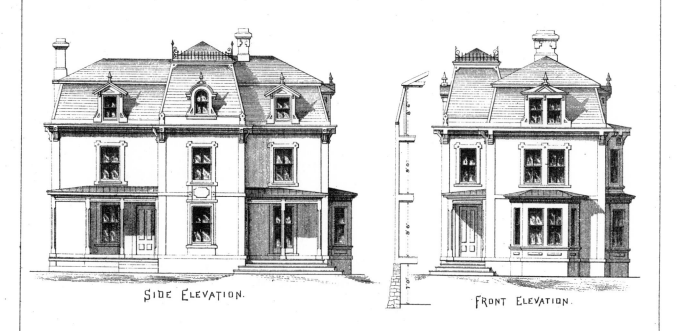

SIDE ELEVATION.　　　　　　　FRONT ELEVATION.

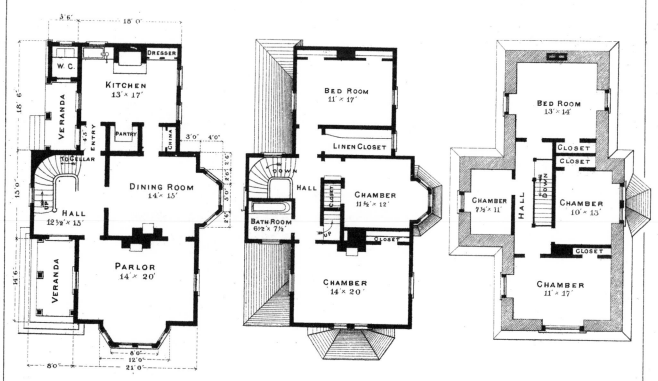

FIRST FLOOR PLAN　　　　　SECOND FLOOR PLAN　　　　　THIRD FLOOR PLAN

SCALE. 1/16 Inch to One Foot.

Design No. 19.

FRONT ELEVATION.

SCALE. 0 3/32 Inch to One Foot.

Engr & print. by. KORFF BROTHERS. 54 William St. N.Y.

Design No. 19.

SIDE ELEVATION.

SCALE. 0 ³/₃₂ Inch to One Foot.

Engr. & print by KORFF BROTHERS. 54 William St. N.Y.

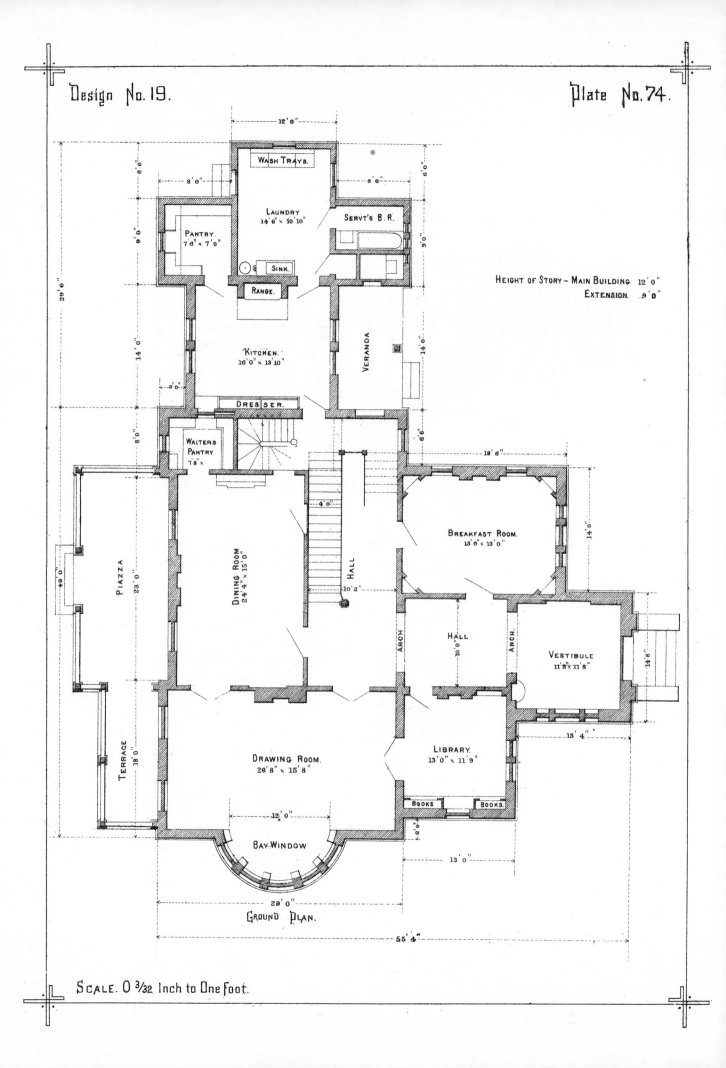

Design No.19.                                    Plate No.74.

12'6"

WASH TRAYS.

8'6"                              8'6"                    6'0"

LAUNDRY
14'6" x 10'10"          SERVT'S B.R.

PANTRY.
7'6" x 7'0"                                              9'0"

SINK.

RANGE.

HEIGHT OF STORY — MAIN BUILDING 12'0"
EXTENSION  9'0"

KITCHEN.
16'0" x 13'10"          VERANDA          14'0"

DRESSER.

WAITERS
PANTRY
7'8"                                          18'6"

4'0"

BREAKFAST ROOM.
13'6" x 13'0"                        14'0"

PIAZZA
23'0"          DINING ROOM.
24'4" x 15'0"          HALL          ARCH          HALL
10'0"          ARCH          VESTIBULE
11'8" x 11'8"

10'2"

13'4"

TERRACE
18'0"          DRAWING ROOM.
26'8" x 15'8"          LIBRARY.
13'0" x 11'9"

BOOKS.          BOOKS.

12'0"                              13'0"

BAY WINDOW

29'0"

GROUND PLAN.

55'4"

SCALE. O 3/32 Inch to One Foot.

Design No. 19. Plate No. 75.

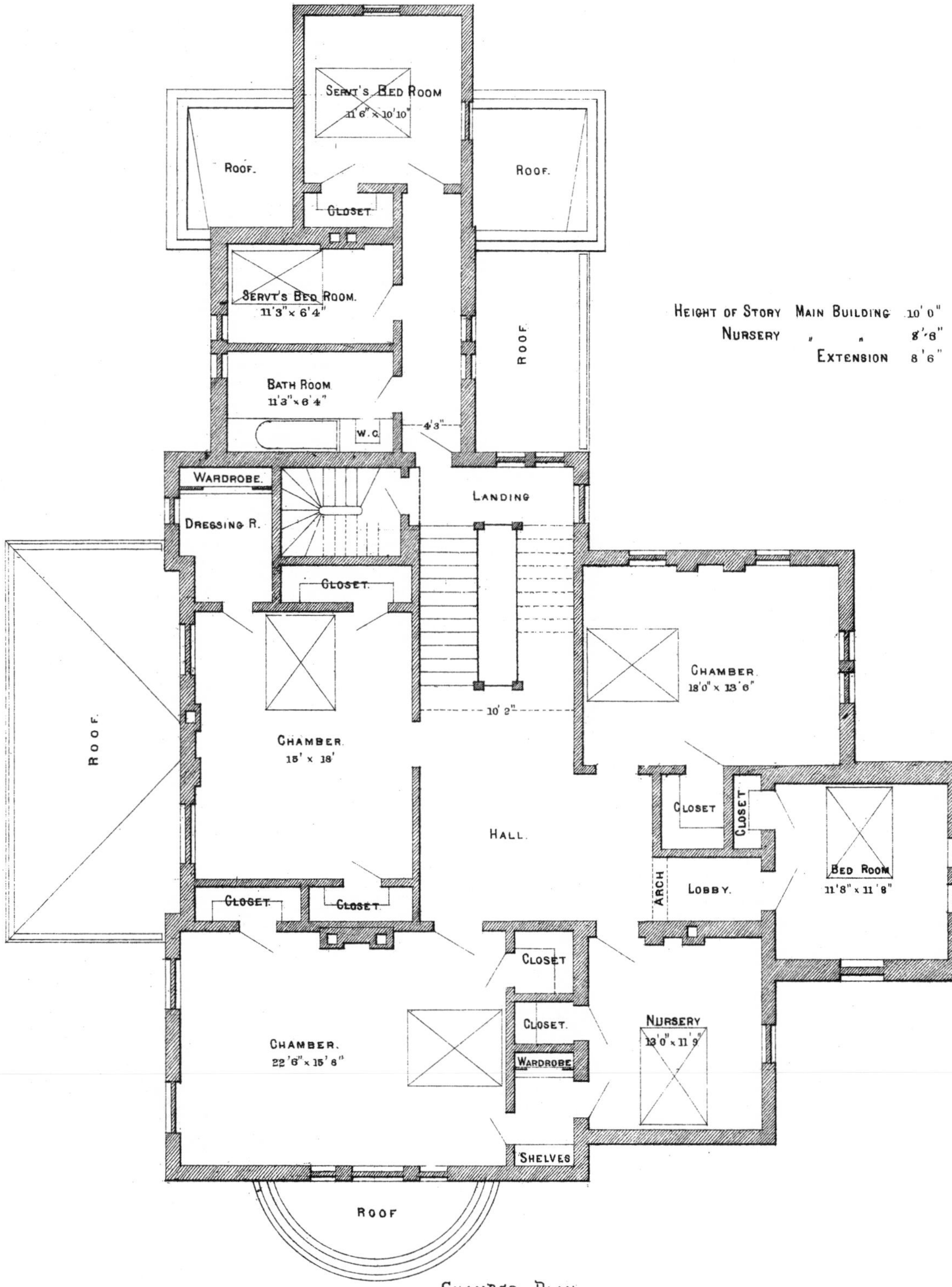
Servt's Bed Room
11'6" × 10'10"
Roof.
Roof.
Closet
Servt's Bed Room.
11'3" × 6'4"
Roof
Bath Room
11'3" × 6'4"
W.C.
4'3"
Height of Story Main Building 10'0"
Nursery " " 8'6"
Extension 8'6"
Wardrobe.
Landing
Dressing R.
Closet.
Chamber
18'0" × 13'6"
Roof
10'2"
Chamber.
15' × 18'
Closet
Closet
Hall.
Bed Room
11'8" × 11'8"
Arch
Lobby.
Closet.
Closet.
Closet
Closet.
Nursery
13'0" × 11'9"
Chamber.
22'6" × 15'6"
Wardrobe
Shelves
Roof

Chamber Plan.

Scale. 0 3/32 Inch to One Foot.

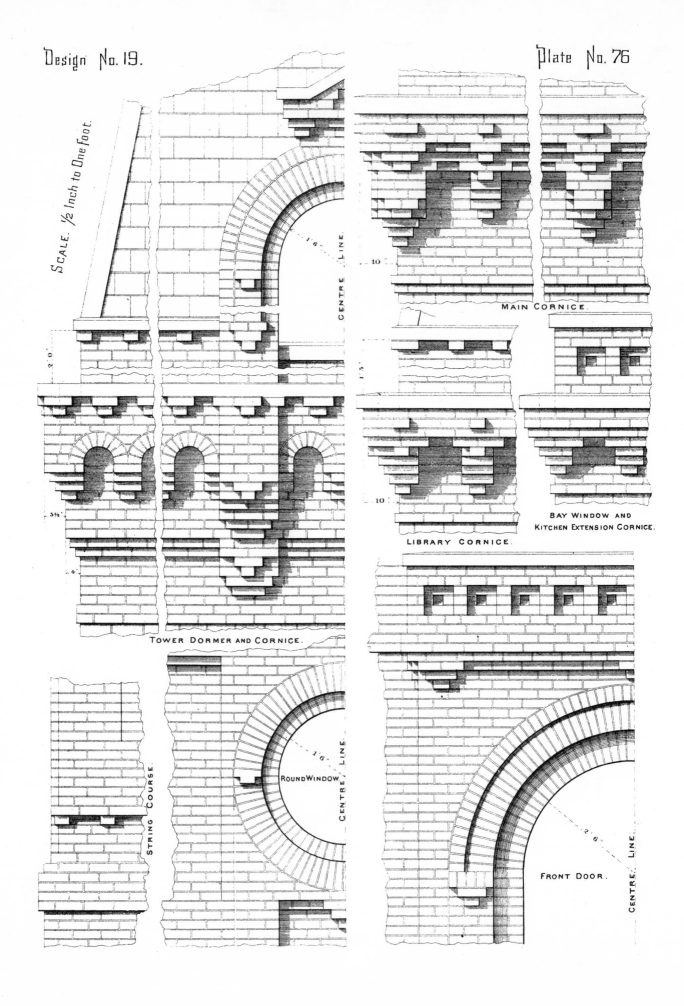

Design No. 19.

Plate No. 76

Scale. ½ Inch to One foot.

CENTRE LINE.

TOWER DORMER AND CORNICE.

STRING COURSE.

Round Window.

CENTRE LINE.

MAIN CORNICE.

LIBRARY CORNICE.

BAY WINDOW AND
KITCHEN EXTENSION CORNICE.

FRONT DOOR.

CENTRE LINE.

Design No. 19.                                    Plate No. 77.

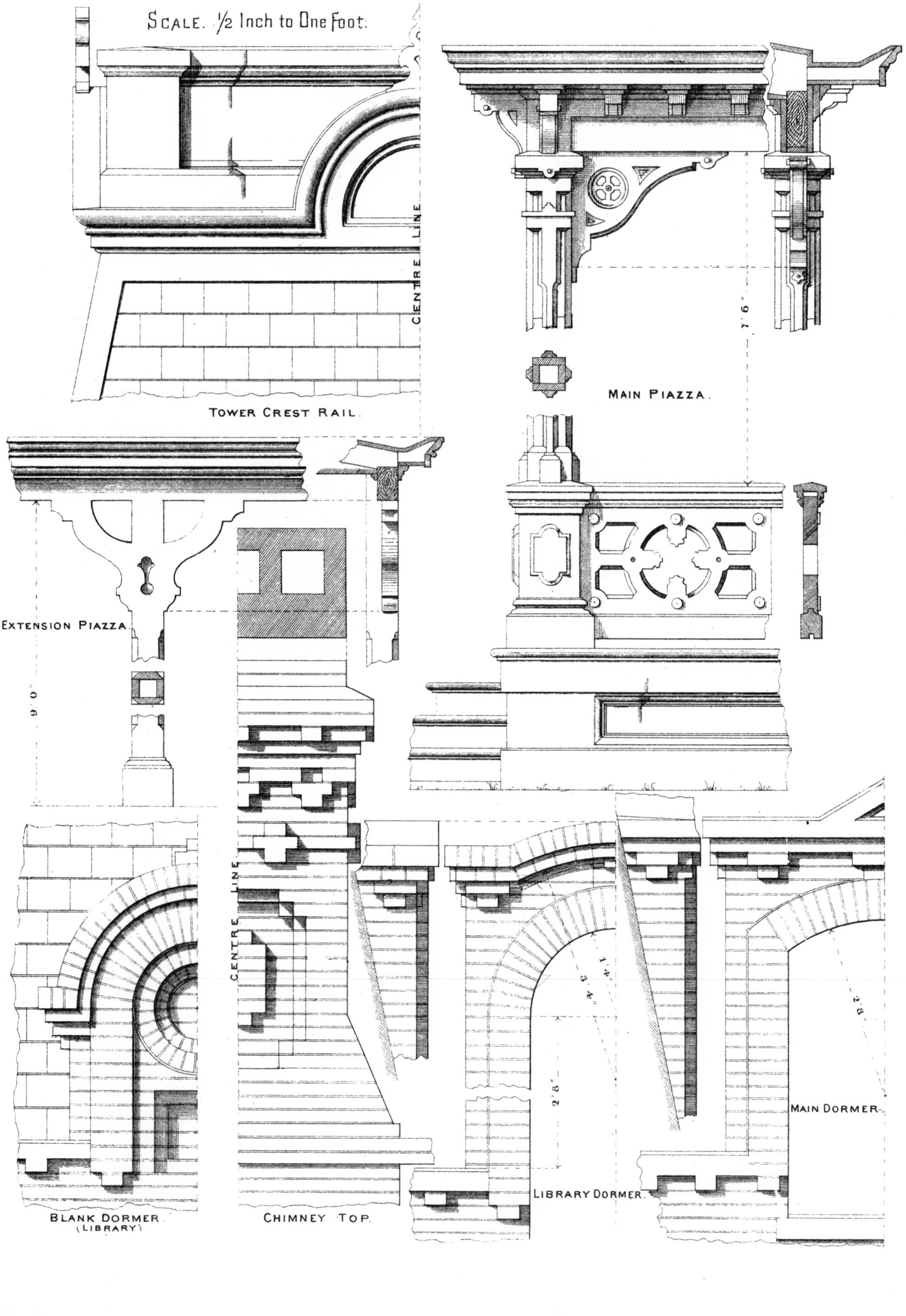

SCALE. ½ Inch to One Foot:

CENTRE LINE

TOWER CREST RAIL.

MAIN PIAZZA.

EXTENSION PIAZZA

9' 0"

7' 6"

CENTRE LINE

BLANK DORMER
(LIBRARY)

CHIMNEY TOP.

LIBRARY DORMER.

MAIN DORMER.

2' 8"

3' 4"

1' 4"

2' 8"

Design No. 20.

Plate No. 78.

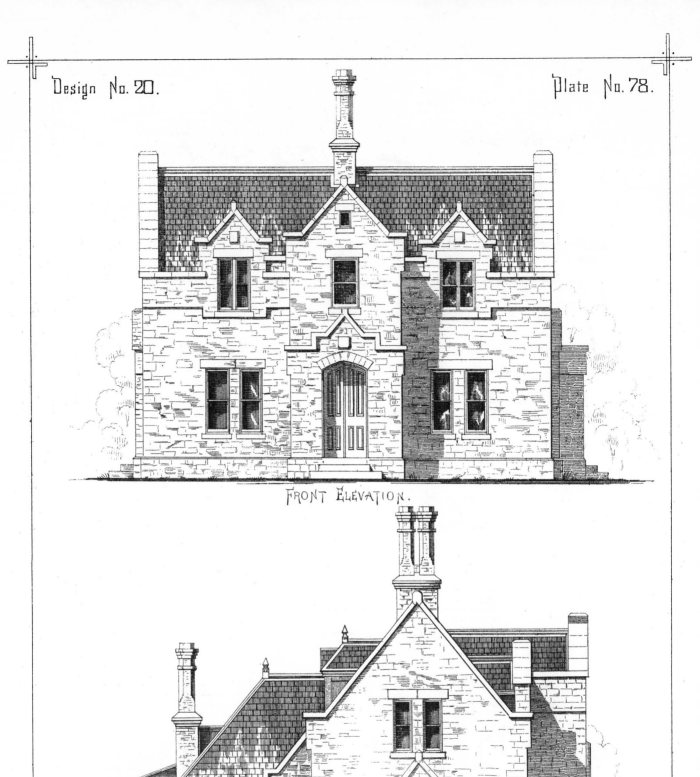

FRONT ELEVATION.

SIDE ELEVATION.

SCALE 0'/8 IN TO ONE FOOT.

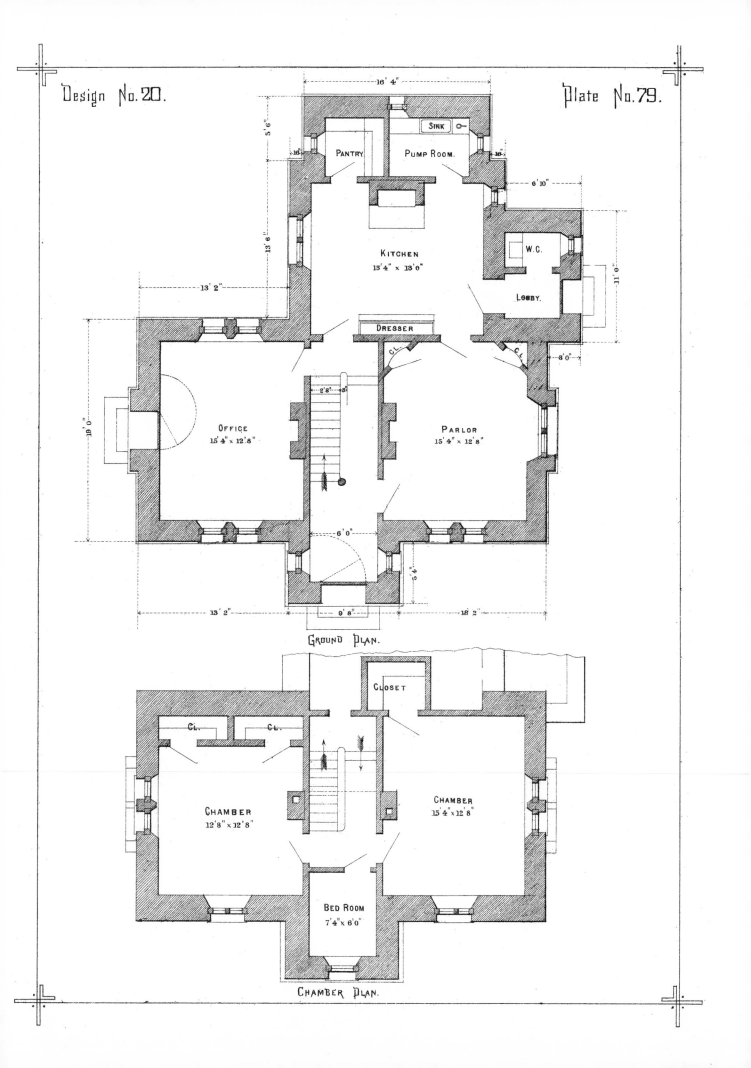

Design No. 20.                    Plate No. 79.

16' 4"

5' 6"

16"    PANTRY    PUMP ROOM.    16"    6' 10"

KITCHEN
15' 4" x 13' 0"    W.C.    11' 0"

13' 6"    LOBBY.

13' 2"    DRESSER    CL.    CL.    3' 0"

2' 8"    8"

19' 0"    OFFICE
15' 4" x 12' 8"    PARLOR
15' 4" x 12' 8"

6' 0"    5' 4"

13' 2"    9' 8"    18' 2"

GROUND PLAN.

CLOSET

CL.    CL.

CHAMBER
12' 8" x 12' 8"    CHAMBER
15' 4" x 12' 8"

BED ROOM
7' 4" x 6' 0"

CHAMBER PLAN.

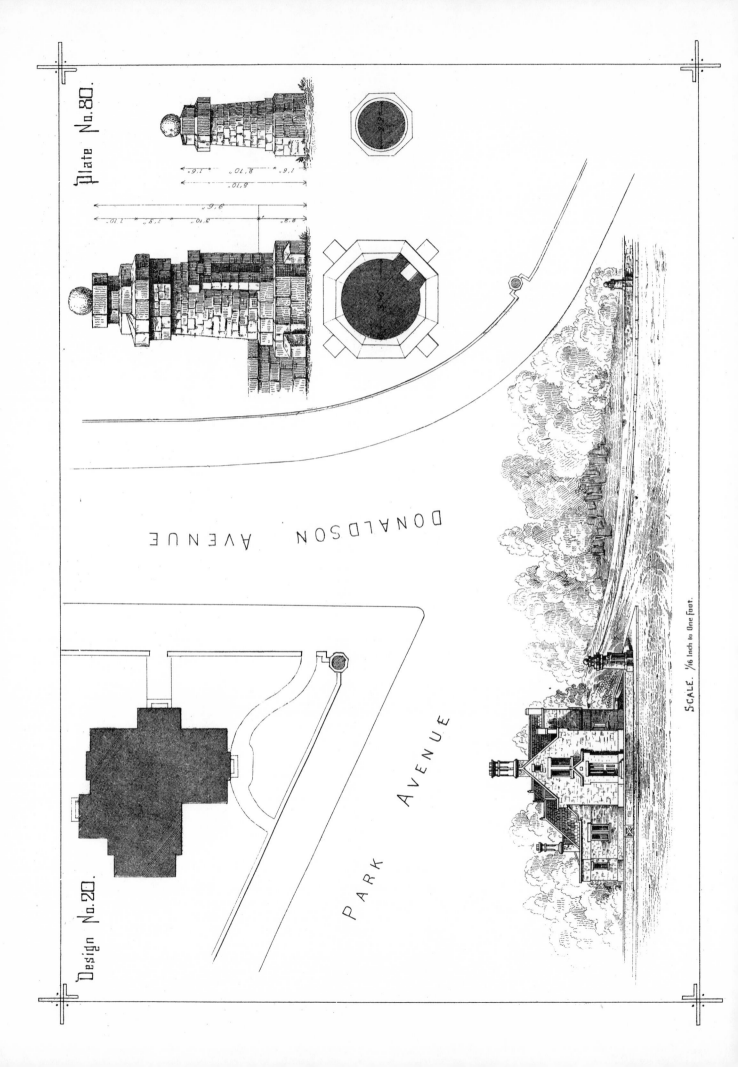

Plate No. 80.

Design No. 20.

DONALDSON AVENUE

PARK AVENUE

SCALE. 1/16 Inch to One Foot.

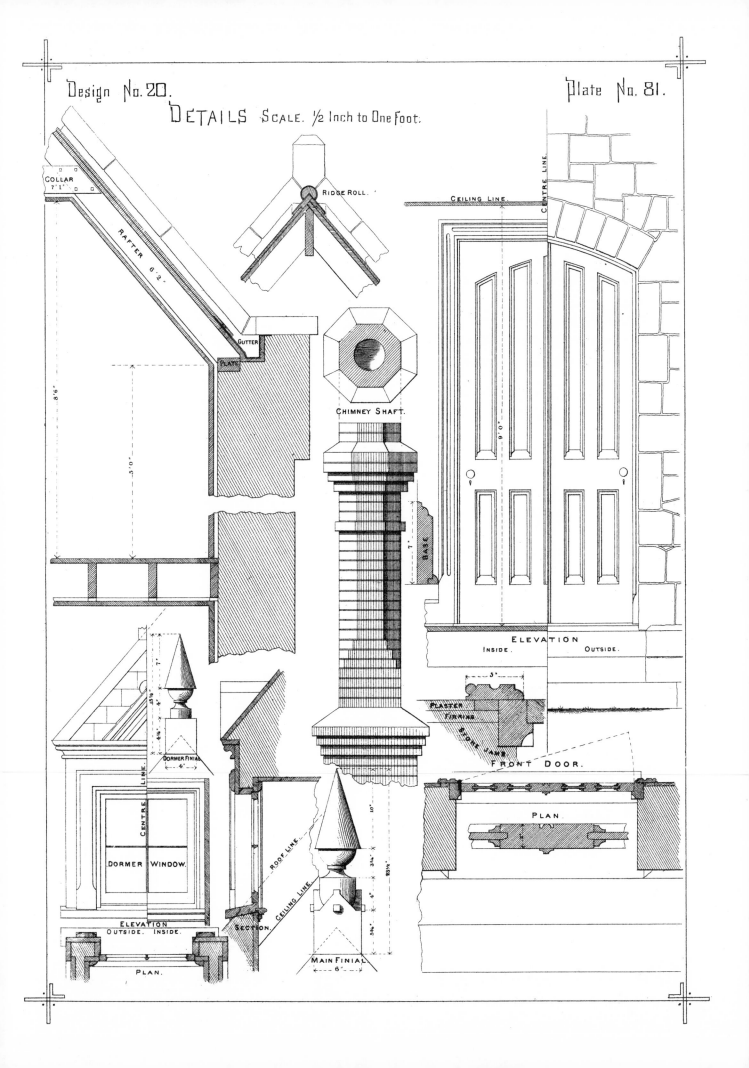

Design No. 20.

Plate No. 81.

DETAILS Scale. ½ Inch to One Foot.

RIDGE ROLL.

COLLAR 7'1"

RAFTER 6'2"

GUTTER

PLATE

8'6"

5'0"

CHIMNEY SHAFT.

CEILING LINE.

CENTRE LINE

BASE

7"

9'0"

ELEVATION

INSIDE.          OUTSIDE.

5"

PLASTER

FIRRING

STONE JAMB

FRONT DOOR.

7"

15⅛"

4½"

DORMER FINIAL

4"

CENTRE LINE

DORMER WINDOW.

ELEVATION

OUTSIDE.  INSIDE.

PLAN.

ROOF LINE.

CEILING LINE.

SECTION.

10"

3½"

23¾"

4"

5½"

MAIN FINIAL

6'

PLAN.

C.

Section at C.

Section at D.

D.

B.

C.

C.

Section on AB

A.

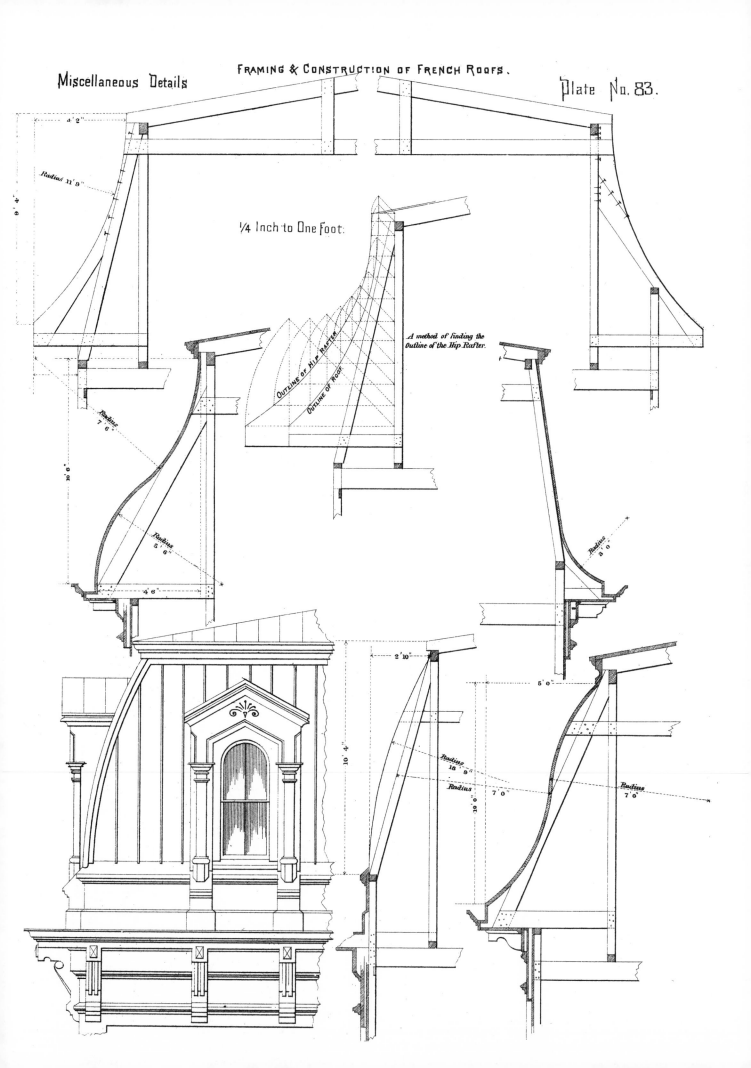

Miscellaneous Details

Plate No. 83.

¼ Inch to One Foot.

A method of finding the
Outline of the Hip Rafter.

OUTLINE OF HIP RAFTER

OUTLINE OF ROOF

Radius 11' 9"

Radius 7' 6"

Radius 5' 6"

Radius 3' 0"

Radius 16' 9"

Radius 7' 0"

Radius 7' 0"

4' 2"

9' 4"

10' 6"

4' 6"

2' 10"

10' 4"

5' 0"

10' 0"

# Miscellaneous Details

DORMER WINDOWS.

¼ Inch to One Foot:

Plate No. 84.

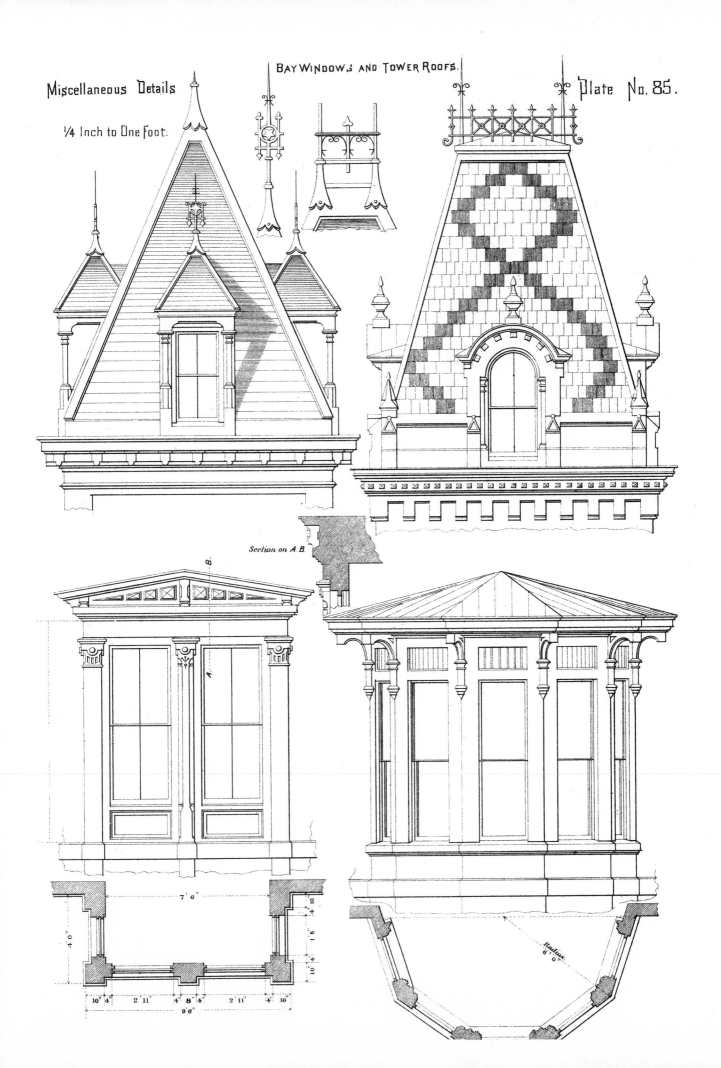

Miscellaneous Details

BAY WINDOWS AND TOWER ROOFS.

Plate No. 85.

¼ Inch to One Foot.

Section on A.B.

B.

A.

7' 6"

4' 0"

4' 10"

8"

4' 10"

10" 4"     2' 11"     4" 8" 4"     2' 11"     4"     10"

9' 6"

Radius 6' 0"

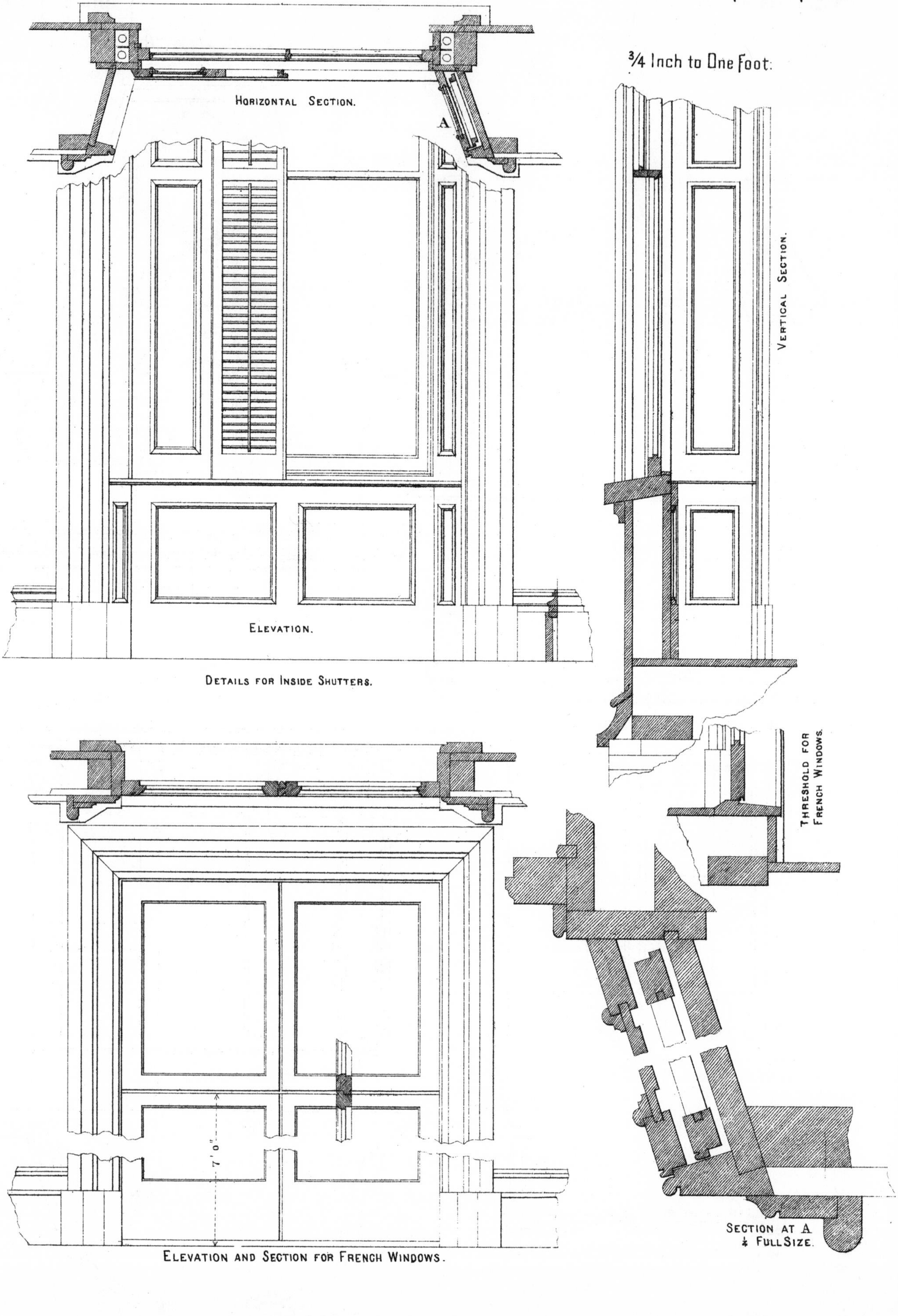

Miscellaneous Details   Inside Shutters & french Window          Plate  No. 86

HORIZONTAL SECTION.

¾ Inch to One Foot:

A

VERTICAL SECTION.

ELEVATION.

DETAILS FOR INSIDE SHUTTERS.

THRESHOLD FOR FRENCH WINDOWS.

7' 0"

ELEVATION AND SECTION FOR FRENCH WINDOWS.

SECTION AT A
¼ FULL SIZE.

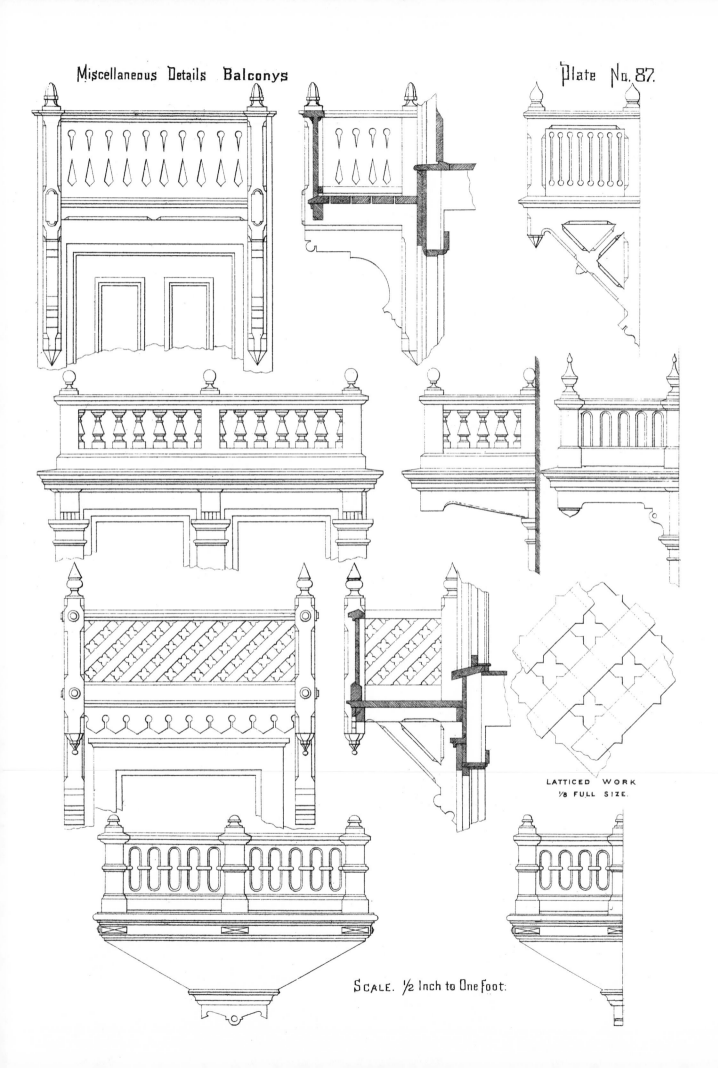

LATTICED WORK
⅛ FULL SIZE.

SCALE. ½ Inch to One Foot.

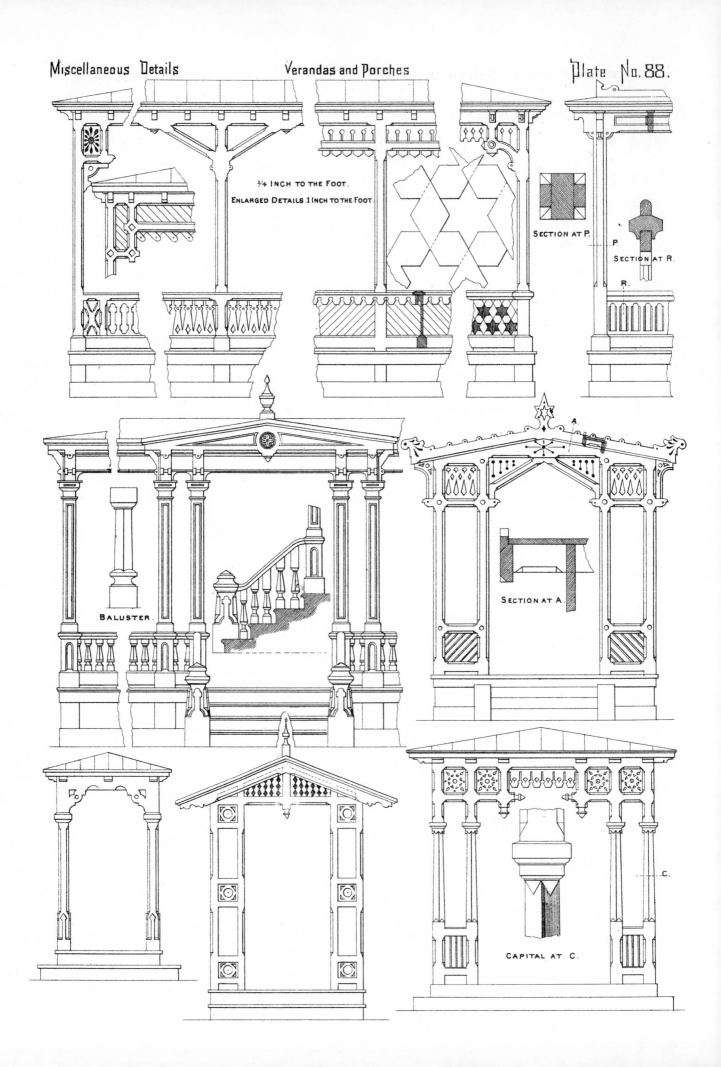

¼ INCH TO THE FOOT.

ENLARGED DETAILS 1 INCH TO THE FOOT.

SECTION AT P.

SECTION AT R.

BALUSTER.

SECTION AT A.

CAPITAL AT C.

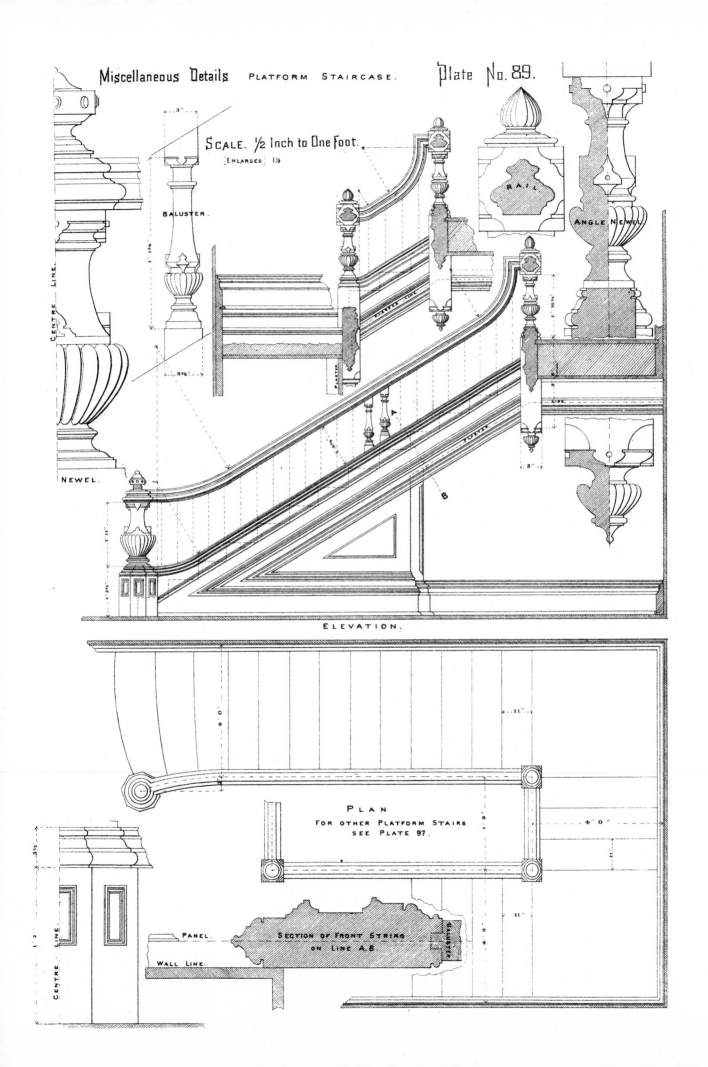

Miscellaneous Details  PLATFORM STAIRCASE.  Plate No. 89.

SCALE. ½ Inch to One Foot.

[ENLARGED] 1½

BALUSTER.

RAIL

ANGLE NEWEL

NEWEL.

ELEVATION.

PLAN
FOR OTHER PLATFORM STAIRS
SEE PLATE 97.

PANEL.

SECTION OF FRONT STRING
ON LINE A.B

BALUSTER

WALL LINE.

CENTRE LINE.

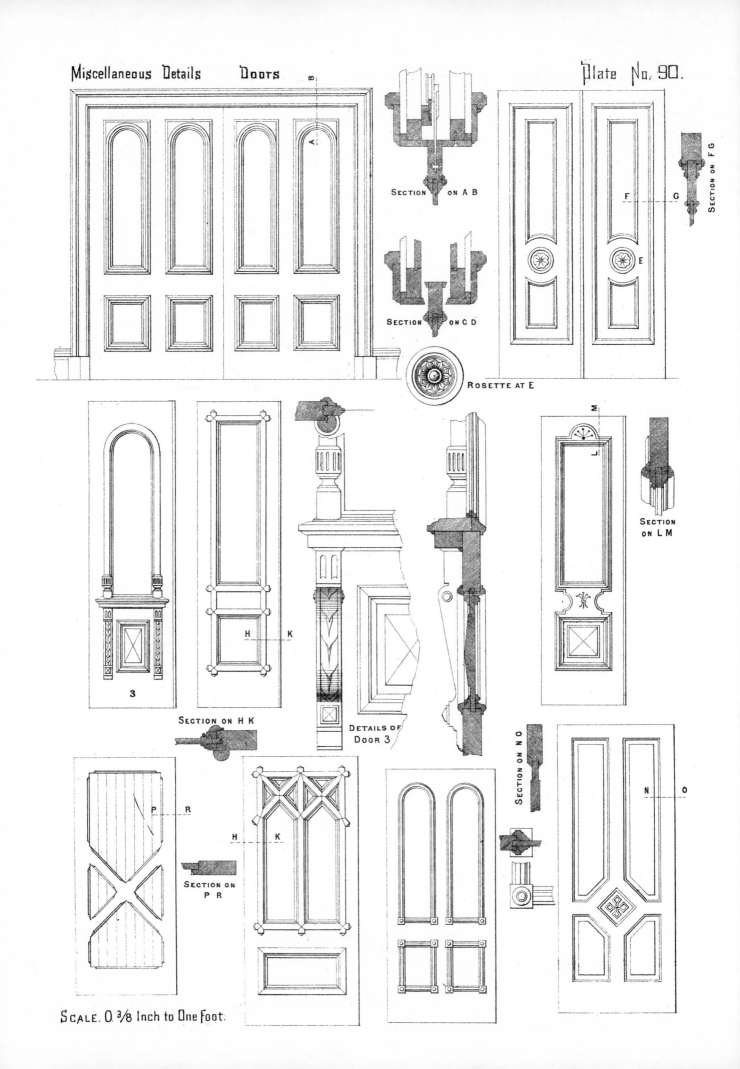

Miscellaneous Details   Doors                                    Plate No. 90.

SECTION ON A B

SECTION ON C D

ROSETTE AT E

SECTION ON F G

SECTION ON L M

3

SECTION ON H K

DETAILS OF DOOR 3

SECTION ON N O

SECTION ON P R

SCALE. 0 3/8 Inch to One Foot.

¼ Inch to One Foot.

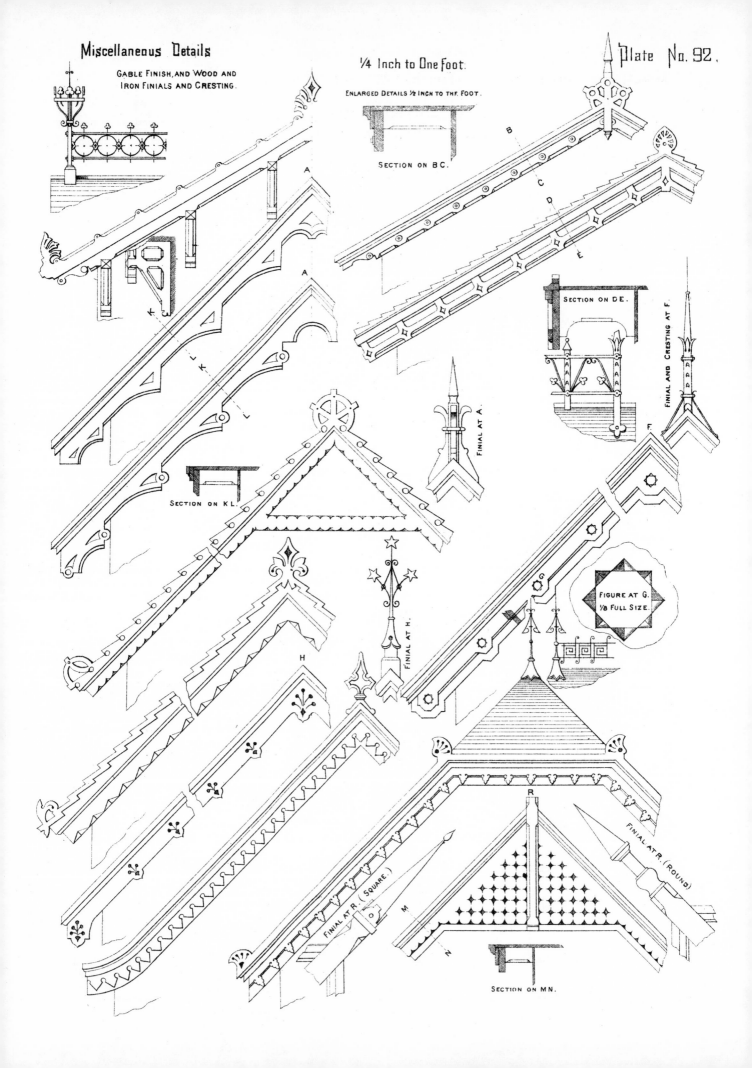

Miscellaneous Details

Gable Finish, and Wood and Iron Finials and Cresting.

¼ Inch to One Foot.

Plate No. 92.

Enlarged Details ½ Inch to the Foot.

Section on BC.

A

A

B

C

D

E

Section on DE.

Finial and Cresting at F.

F

Section on KL.

Finial at A.

Figure at G. ⅛ Full Size.

G

H

Finial at H.

Finial at R. (Square.)

Finial at R. (Round.)

R

M

N

Section on MN.

SCALE OF 1. 2. 3. 4. ¼ INCH TO THE FOOT. _ SCALE OF 5. ⅛ INCH TO THE FOOT. _ SCALE OF REMAINING DESIGNS ⅜ INCH TO THE FOOT.

LETTERS ON ENLARGED DETAILS REFER TO THE SAME LETTERS ON ELEVATIONS.

ENLARGED DETAILS 1½ INCHES TO THE FOOT.

ELEVATION OF DOORS &C. ⅜ INCHES TO THE FOOT.

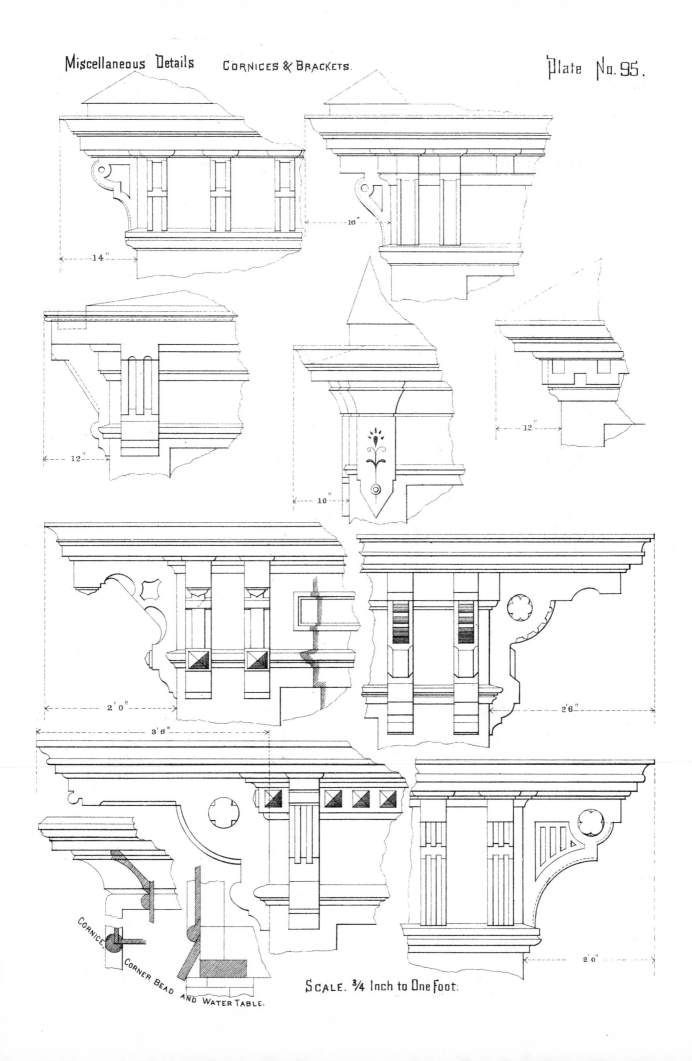

SCALE. ¾ Inch to One Foot.

CORNICE, CORNER BEAD AND WATER TABLE.

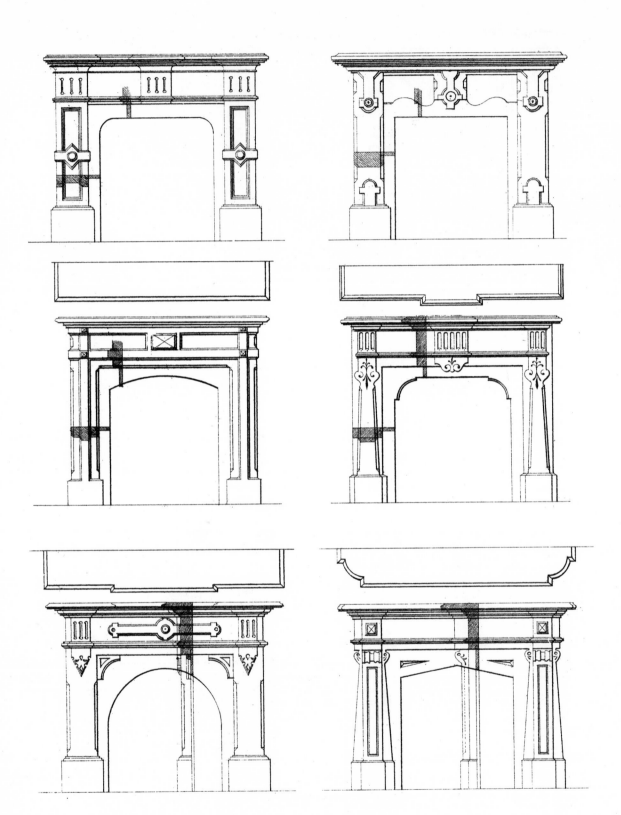

½ Inch to One Foot.

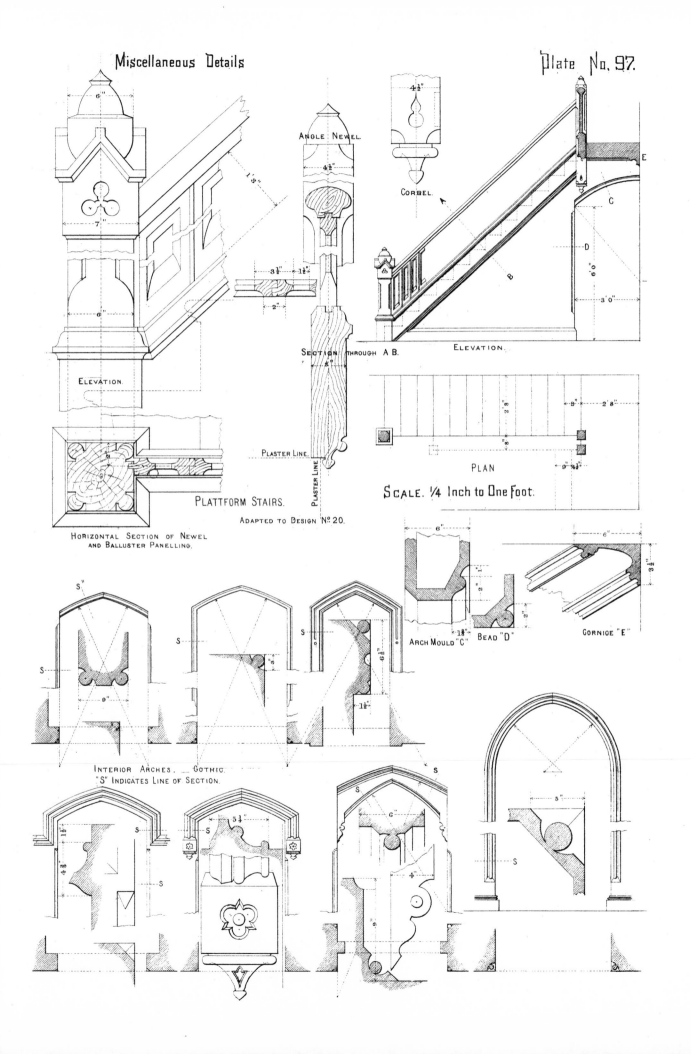

Miscellaneous Details

Plate No. 97.

Angle Newel.

Corbel.

Elevation.

Section through A B.

Plaster Line.

Plattform Stairs.

Adapted to Design Nº 20.

Horizontal Section of Newel
and Balluster Panelling.

Elevation.

Plan

Scale. ¼ Inch to One Foot.

Arch Mould "C". Bead "D". Cornice "E".

Interior Arches. Gothic.
"S" Indicates Line of Section.

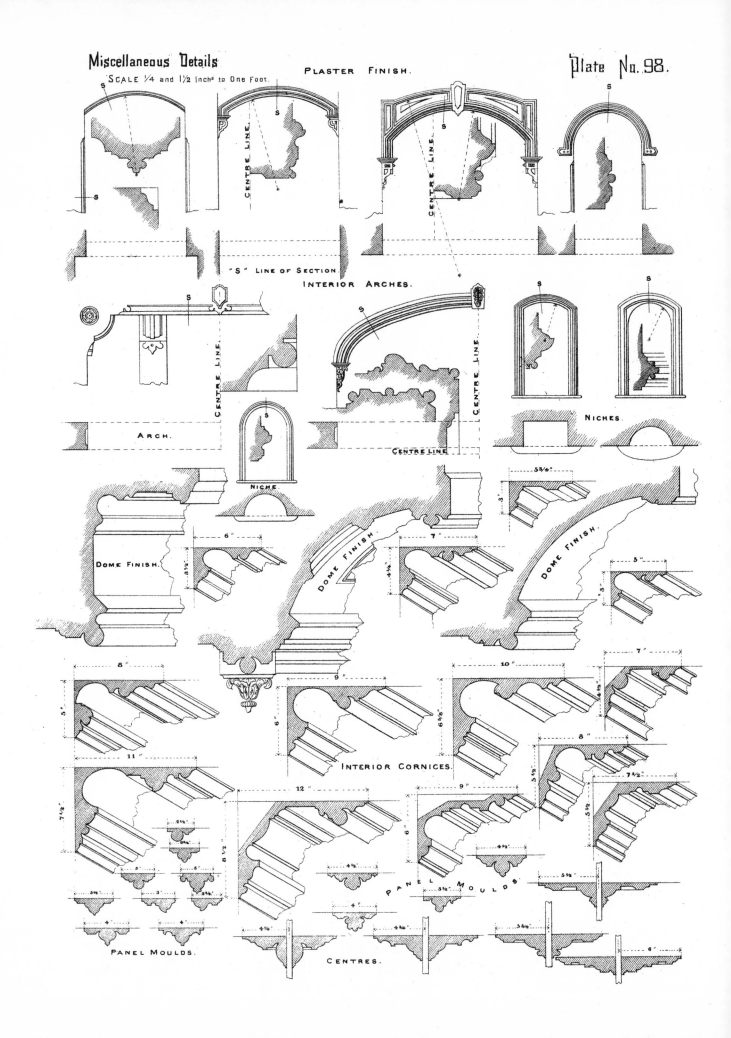

Miscellaneous Details

SCALE ¼ and 1½ Inches to One Foot.

PLASTER FINISH.

Plate No. 98.

CENTRE LINE

CENTRE LINE

CENTRE LINE

"S" LINE OF SECTION.

INTERIOR ARCHES.

CENTRE LINE

CENTRE LINE

ARCH.

CENTRE LINE

NICHES.

NICHE.

DOME FINISH.

DOME FINISH.

DOME FINISH.

INTERIOR CORNICES.

PANEL MOULDS.

PANEL MOULDS.

CENTRES.

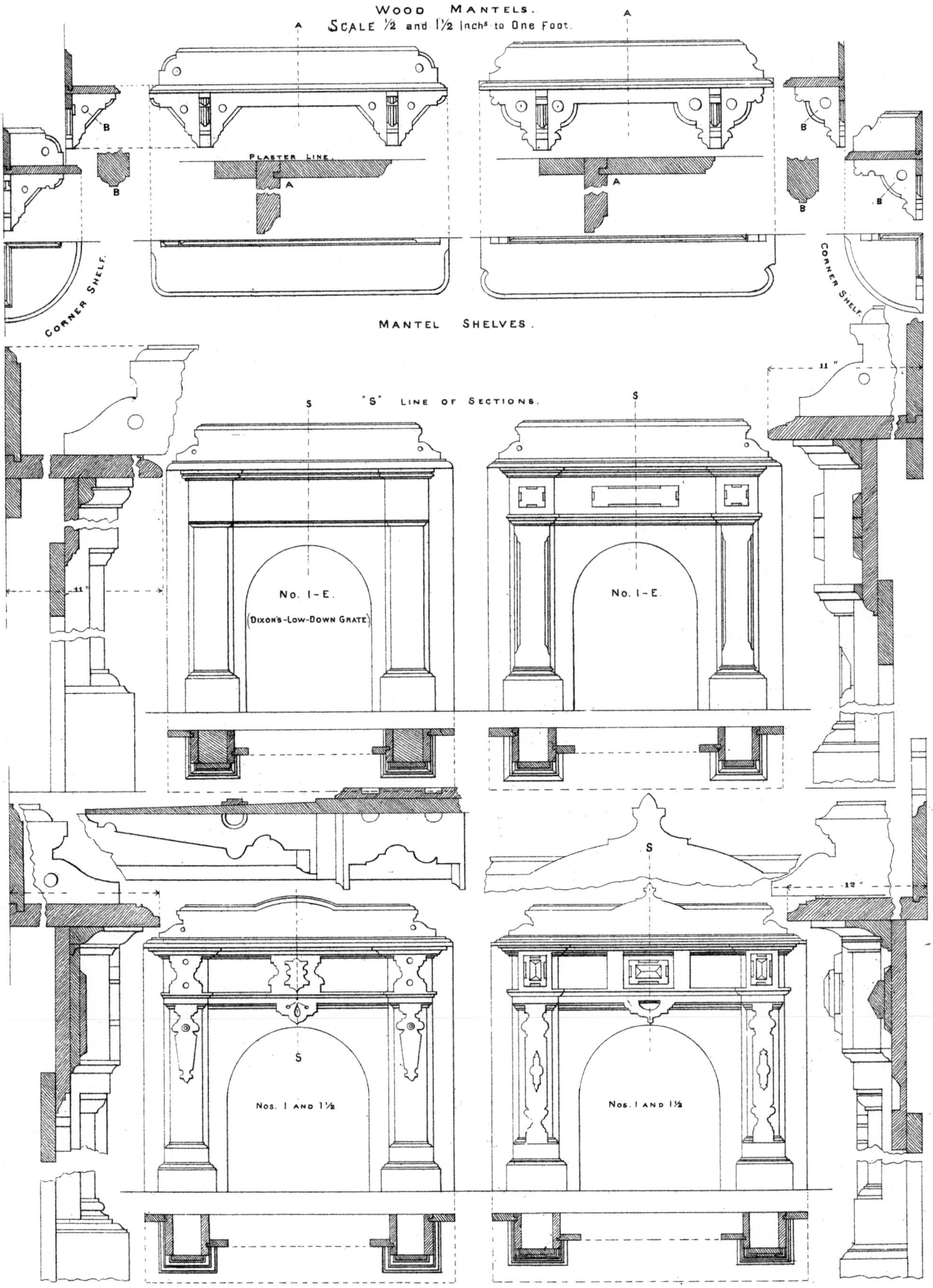
WOOD MANTELS.
SCALE ½ and 1½ Inchs to One Foot.
A
A
B
B
B
B
PLASTER LINE.
A
A
CORNER SHELF.
CORNER SHELF.
MANTEL SHELVES.
"S" LINE OF SECTIONS.
S
S
11"
11"
No. 1-E.
(DIXON'S-LOW-DOWN GRATE)
No. 1-E.
S
12"
S
Nos. 1 AND 1½
Nos. 1 AND 1½

WOOD MANTELS
"S" LINE OF SECTION

SCALE ½ and 1½ Inchs to One Foot.

No. 2

DIXON'S LOW-DOWN GRATE

No. 2

GOTHIC

GOTHIC

No. 2

No. 3

No. 3